MznLnx

Missing Links Exam Preps

Exam Prep for

Intermediate Algebra

Wright, 5th Edition

The MznLnx Exam Prep is your link from the texbook and lecture to your exams.
The MznLnx Exam Preps are unauthorized and comprehensive reviews of your textbooks.

All material provided by MznLnx and Rico Publications (c) 2010
Textbook publishers and textbook authors do not particpate in or contribute to these reviews.

MznLnx

Rico
Publications

Exam Prep for Intermediate Algebra
5th Edition
Wright

Publisher: Raymond Houge
Assistant Editor: Michael Rouger
Text and Cover Designer: Lisa Buckner
Marketing Manager: Sara Swagger
Project Manager, Editorial Production: Jerry Emerson
Art Director: Vernon Lowerui

Product Manager: Dave Mason
Editorial Assitant: Rachel Guzmanji
Pedagogy: Debra Long
Cover Image: Jim Reed/Getty Images
Text and Cover Printer: City Printing, Inc.
Compositor: Media Mix, Inc.

(c) 2010 Rico Publications
ALL RIGHTS RESERVED. No part of this work
covered by the copyright may be reproduced or
used in any form or by an means--graphic, electronic,
or mechanical, including photocopying, recording,
taping, Web distribution, information storage, and
retrieval systems, or in any other manner--without the
written permission of the publisher.

Printed in the United States
ISBN:

For more information about our products, contact us at:

Dave.Mason@RicoPublications.com

For permission to use material from this text or

product, submit a request online to:

Dave.Mason@RicoPublications.com

Contents

CHAPTER 1
Real Numbers, Solving Equations, and Exponents — 1

CHAPTER 2
Straight Lines and Functions — 18

CHAPTER 3
Systems of Linear Equations — 26

CHAPTER 4
Polynomials — 38

CHAPTER 5
Rational Expressions — 51

CHAPTER 6
Roots, Radicals and Complex Numbers — 63

CHAPTER 7
Quadratic Equations — 74

CHAPTER 8
Quadratic Functions and Conic Sections — 86

CHAPTER 9
Exponential and Logarithmic Functions — 98

CHAPTER 10
Sequences, Series, and the Binomial Theorem — 111

ANSWER KEY — 114

TO THE STUDENT

COMPREHENSIVE

The *MznLnx* Exam Prep series is designed to help you pass your exams. Editors at MznLnx review your textbooks and then prepare these practice exams to help you master the textbook material. Unlike study guides, workbooks, and practice tests provided by the texbook publisher and textbook authors, *MznLnx* gives you **all** of the material in each chapter in exam form, not just samples, so you can be sure to nail your exam.

MECHANICAL

The MznLnx Exam Prep series creates exams that will help you learn the subject matter as well as test you on your understanding. Each question is designed to help you master the concept. Just working through the exams, you gain an understanding of the subject--its a simple mechanical process that produces success.

INTEGRATED STUDY GUIDE AND REVIEW

MznLnx is not just a set of exams designed to test you, its also a comprehensive review of the subject content. Each exam question is also a review of the concept, making sure that you will get the answer correct without having to go to other sources of material. You learn as you go! Its the easiest way to pass an exam.

HUMOR

Studying can be tedious and dry. MznLnx's instructional design includes moderate humor within the exam questions on occassion, to break the tedium and revitalize the brain

Chapter 1. Real Numbers, Solving Equations, and Exponents

1. _____ is a mathematical operation, written a^n, involving two numbers, the base a and the exponent n.
   a. Exponentiating0
   b. Thing
   c. Undefined
   d. Undefined

2. _____ is a mathematical operation, written a^n, involving two numbers, the base a and the exponent n.
   a. Exponentiation0
   b. Thing
   c. Undefined
   d. Undefined

3. _____ is a branch of mathematics concerning the study of structure, relation and quantity.
   a. Algebra0
   b. Concept
   c. Undefined
   d. Undefined

4. _____ are the basic objects of study in graph theory. Informally speaking, a graph is a set of objects called points, nodes, or vertices connected by links called lines or edges.
   a. Thing
   b. Graphs0
   c. Undefined
   d. Undefined

5. Mathematical _____ is used to represent ideas.
   a. Thing
   b. Notation0
   c. Undefined
   d. Undefined

6. In elementary algebra, an _____ is a set that contains every real number between two indicated numbers and may contain the two numbers themselves.
   a. Interval0
   b. Thing
   c. Undefined
   d. Undefined

7. _____ is the notation in which permitted values for a variable are expressed as ranging over a certain interval; "5 < x < 9" is an example of the application of _____.
   a. Interval notation0
   b. Thing
   c. Undefined
   d. Undefined

8. A _____ is a one-dimensional picture in which the integers are shown as specially-marked points evenly spaced on a line.
   a. Number line0
   b. Thing
   c. Undefined
   d. Undefined

9. In mathematics, a _____ may be described informally as a number that can be given by an infinite decimal representation.
   a. Thing
   b. Real number0
   c. Undefined
   d. Undefined

10. In common philosophical language, a proposition or _____, is the content of an assertion, that is, it is true-or-false and defined by the meaning of a particular piece of language.
    a. Concept
    b. Statement0
    c. Undefined
    d. Undefined

11. A _____ is a number that is less than zero.

Chapter 1. Real Numbers, Solving Equations, and Exponents

    a. Thing
    c. Undefined
    b. Negative number0
    d. Undefined

12. _____ or arithmetics is the oldest and most elementary branch of mathematics, used by almost everyone, for tasks ranging from simple daily counting to advanced science and business calculations.
    a. Arithmetic0
    c. Undefined
    b. Thing
    d. Undefined

13. The _____ are the only integral domain whose positive elements are well-ordered, and in which order is preserved by addition. Like the natural numbers, the _____ form a countably infinite set. The set of all _____ is usually denoted in mathematics by a boldface Z .
    a. Thing
    c. Undefined
    b. Integers0
    d. Undefined

14. In mathematics, a _____ number is a number which can be expressed as a ratio of two integers. Non-integer _____ numbers (commonly called fractions) are usually written as the vulgar fraction a / b, where b is not zero.
    a. Rational0
    c. Undefined
    b. Thing
    d. Undefined

15. In mathematics, the additive inverse, or _____ of a number n is the number that, when added to n, yields zero. The additive inverse of n is denoted −n. For example, 7 is −7, because 7 + (−7) = 0, and the additive inverse of −0.3 is 0.3, because −0.3 + 0.3 = 0.
    a. Opposite0
    c. Undefined
    b. Thing
    d. Undefined

16. In mathematics, an _____ number is any real number that is not a rational number- that is, it is a number which cannot be expressed as a fraction m/n, where m and n are integers.
    a. Irrational0
    c. Undefined
    b. Thing
    d. Undefined

17. In mathematics, an _____ is any real number that is not a rational number ¡ª that is, it is a number which cannot be expressed as m/n, where m and n are integers.
    a. Thing
    c. Undefined
    b. Irrational number0
    d. Undefined

18. In mathematics, _____ are any real number that is not a rational number ¡ª that is, it is a number which cannot be expressed as m/n, where m and n are integers.
    a. Irrational numbers0
    c. Undefined
    b. Thing
    d. Undefined

19. _____ is the state of being greater than any finite real or natural number, however large.
    a. Thing
    c. Undefined
    b. Infinite0
    d. Undefined

20. A _____ decimal is a number whose decimal representation eventually becomes periodic (i.e. the same number sequence _____ indefinitely).

Chapter 1. Real Numbers, Solving Equations, and Exponents

a. Thing
b. Repeating0
c. Undefined
d. Undefined

21. A _____ decimal is a decimal fraction which ends after a definite number of digits.
   a. Terminating0
   b. Thing
   c. Undefined
   d. Undefined

22. Leonhard _____ was a pioneering Swiss mathematician and physicist, who spent most of his life in Russia and Germany.
   a. Person
   b. Euler0
   c. Undefined
   d. Undefined

23. _____ was a pioneering Swiss mathematician and physicist, who spent most of his life in Russia and Germany.
   a. Leonhard Euler0
   b. Person
   c. Undefined
   d. Undefined

24. In mathematics, a _____ can mean either an element of the set {1, 2, 3, ...} (i.e the positive integers or the counting numbers) or an element of the set {0, 1, 2, 3, ...} (i.e. the non-negative integers).
   a. Natural number0
   b. Thing
   c. Undefined
   d. Undefined

25. In mathematics, a _____ can mean either an element of the set {1, 2, 3, ...} (i.e the positive integers) or an element of the set {0, 1, 2, 3, ...} (i.e. the non-negative integers).
   a. Whole number0
   b. Concept
   c. Undefined
   d. Undefined

26. In plane geometry, a _____ is a polygon with four equal sides, four right angles, and parallel opposite sides. In algebra, the _____ of a number is that number multiplied by itself.
   a. Square0
   b. Thing
   c. Undefined
   d. Undefined

27. In mathematics, a _____ of a number x is a number r such that $r^2 = x$, or in words, a number r whose square (the result of multiplying the number by itself) is x.
   a. Square root0
   b. Thing
   c. Undefined
   d. Undefined

28. _____ is the calculated approximation of a result which is usable even if input data may be incomplete, uncertain, or noisy.
   a. Concept
   b. Estimation0
   c. Undefined
   d. Undefined

29. The term _____ can refer to an integer which is the square of some other integer, or an algebraic expression that can be factored as the square of some other expression.
   a. Thing
   b. Perfect square0
   c. Undefined
   d. Undefined

30. In mathematics, a _____ of a complex-valued function f is a member x of the domain of f such that f(x) vanishes at x, that is, x : f (x) = 0.
   a. Thing
   b. Root0
   c. Undefined
   d. Undefined

31. The _____ of measurement are a globally standardized and modernized form of the metric system.
   a. Units0
   b. Thing
   c. Undefined
   d. Undefined

32. In Euclidean geometry, a _____ is the set of all points in a plane at a fixed distance, called the radius, from a given point, the center.
   a. Thing
   b. Circle0
   c. Undefined
   d. Undefined

33. The _____ is the distance around a closed curve. _____ is a kind of perimeter.
   a. Circumference0
   b. Thing
   c. Undefined
   d. Undefined

34. In geometry, a _____ (Greek words diairo = divide and metro = measure) of a circle is any straight line segment that passes through the centre and whose endpoints are on the circular boundary, or, in more modern usage, the length of such a line segment. When using the word in the more modern sense, one speaks of the _____ rather than a _____, because all diameters of a circle have the same length. This length is twice the radius. The _____ of a circle is also the longest chord that the circle has.
   a. Thing
   b. Diameter0
   c. Undefined
   d. Undefined

35. An _____ or member of a set is an object that when collected together make up the set.
   a. Thing
   b. Element0
   c. Undefined
   d. Undefined

36. In mathematics, the _____ , or members of a set or more generally a class are all those objects which when collected together make up the set or class.
   a. Thing
   b. Elements0
   c. Undefined
   d. Undefined

37. In mathematics and more specifically set theory, the _____ set is the unique set which contains no elements.
   a. Empty0
   b. Thing
   c. Undefined
   d. Undefined

38. In measure theory, a _____ is a set that is negligible for the purposes of the measure in question.
   a. Null set0
   b. Concept
   c. Undefined
   d. Undefined

39. _____ is the chance that something is likely to happen or be the case.

a. Probability0
b. Thing
c. Undefined
d. Undefined

40. _____ is a mathematical science pertaining to the collection, analysis, interpretation or explanation, and presentation of data. It is applicable to a wide variety of academic disciplines, from the physical and social sciences to the humanities.
    a. Thing
    b. Statistics0
    c. Undefined
    d. Undefined

41. In mathematics, the _____ of two sets A and B is the set that contains all elements of A that also belong to B (or equivalently, all elements of B that also belong to A), but no other elements.
    a. Intersection0
    b. Thing
    c. Undefined
    d. Undefined

42. In set theory and other branches of mathematics, the _____ of a collection of sets is the set that contains everything that belongs to any of the sets, but nothing else.
    a. Union0
    b. Thing
    c. Undefined
    d. Undefined

43. In mathematics, an _____ is a statement about the relative size or order of two objects.
    a. Inequality0
    b. Thing
    c. Undefined
    d. Undefined

44. In mathematics, _____ is an elementary arithmetic operation. When one of the numbers is a whole number, _____ is the repeated sum of the other number.
    a. Multiplication0
    b. Thing
    c. Undefined
    d. Undefined

45. An _____ is an equality that remains true regardless of the values of any variables that appear within it, to distinguish it from an equality which is true under more particular conditions.
    a. Thing
    b. Identity0
    c. Undefined
    d. Undefined

46. In mathematics, the _____ inverse, or opposite, of a number n is the number that, when added to n, yields zero. The _____ inverse of n is denoted −n.
    a. Thing
    b. Additive0
    c. Undefined
    d. Undefined

47. In mathematics the _____ of a set which is equipped with the operation of addition is an element which, when added to any other element x in the set, yields x.
    a. Concept
    b. Additive identity0
    c. Undefined
    d. Undefined

48. In mathematics, the _____ inverse of a number x, denoted 1/x or x^{-1}, is the number which, when multiplied by x, yields 1. The _____ inverse of x is also called the reciprocal of x.

Chapter 1. Real Numbers, Solving Equations, and Exponents

a. Thing
b. Multiplicative0
c. Undefined
d. Undefined

49. In mathematics, _____ is a property that a binary operation can have. Within an expression containing two or more of the same associative operators in a row, the order of operations does not matter as long as the sequence of the operands is not changed.
    a. Thing
    b. Associativity0
    c. Undefined
    d. Undefined

50. In mathematics, defined and _____ are used to explain whether or not expressions have meaningful, sensible, and unambiguous values.
    a. Thing
    b. Undefined0
    c. Undefined
    d. Undefined

51. In mathematics, the _____ of a number x, denoted 1/x or x^{-1}, is the number which, when multiplied by x, yields 1. The _____ of x is also called the reciprocal of x.
    a. Multiplicative inverse0
    b. Thing
    c. Undefined
    d. Undefined

52. _____ element of an element x with respect to a binary operation * with identity element e is an element y such that x * y = y * x = e. In particular,
    a. Thing
    b. Inverse0
    c. Undefined
    d. Undefined

53. In mathematics, an inequality is a statement about the relative size or order of two objects. For example 14 > 10, or 14 is _____ 10.
    a. Thing
    b. Greater than0
    c. Undefined
    d. Undefined

54. The _____ is a property of multiplication or addition where the product or sum remains the same, regardless of whether or not the order of the addends or factors are changed.
    a. Commutative property0
    b. Thing
    c. Undefined
    d. Undefined

55. In mathematics, and in particular in abstract algebra, the _____ is a property of binary operations that generalises the distributive law from elementary algebra.
    a. Distributive property0
    b. Thing
    c. Undefined
    d. Undefined

56. A _____ is a symbolic representation denoting a quantity or expression. It often represents an "unknown" quantity that has the potential to change.
    a. Variable0
    b. Thing
    c. Undefined
    d. Undefined

57. A _____ is the part of a fraction that tells how many equal parts make up a whole, and which is used in the name of the fraction: "halves", "thirds", "fourths" or "quarters", "fifths" and so on.

Chapter 1. Real Numbers, Solving Equations, and Exponents

a. Denominator0
b. Concept
c. Undefined
d. Undefined

58. An _____ is a combination of numbers, operators, grouping symbols and/or free variables and bound variables arranged in a meaningful way which can be evaluated..
    a. Expression0
    b. Thing
    c. Undefined
    d. Undefined

59. In mathematics, the _____ (or modulus) of a real number is its numerical value without regard to its sign.
    a. Absolute value0
    b. Thing
    c. Undefined
    d. Undefined

60. In arithmetic and algebra, when a number or expression is both preceded and followed by a binary operation, an _____ is required for which operation should be applied first.
    a. Thing
    b. Order of operations0
    c. Undefined
    d. Undefined

61. A _____ is a set of possible values that a variable can take on in order to satisfy a given set of conditions, which may include equations and inequalities.
    a. Solution set0
    b. Thing
    c. Undefined
    d. Undefined

62. The _____ integers are all the integers from zero on upwards.
    a. Nonnegative0
    b. Thing
    c. Undefined
    d. Undefined

63. A frame of _____ is a particular perspective from which the universe is observed.
    a. Reference0
    b. Thing
    c. Undefined
    d. Undefined

64. A _____ is the result of the addition of a set of numbers. The numbers may be natural numbers, complex numbers, matrices, or still more complicated objects. An infinite _____ is a subtle procedure known as a series.
    a. Thing
    b. Sum0
    c. Undefined
    d. Undefined

65. In mathematics, the _____ of a number n is the number that, when added to n, yields zero. The _____ of n is denoted −n. For example, 7 is −7, because 7 + (−7) = 0, and the _____ of −0.3 is 0.3, because −0.3 + 0.3 = 0.
    a. Additive inverse0
    b. Thing
    c. Undefined
    d. Undefined

66. In topology and related areas of mathematics a _____ or Moore-Smith sequence is a generalization of a sequence, intended to unify the various notions of limit and generalize them to arbitrary topological spaces.
    a. Net0
    b. Thing
    c. Undefined
    d. Undefined

Chapter 1. Real Numbers, Solving Equations, and Exponents

67. In mathematics, the conjugate _____ or adjoint matrix of an m-by-n matrix A with complex entries is the n-by-m matrix A* obtained from A by taking the transpose and then taking the complex conjugate of each entry.
    a. Pairs0
    b. Thing
    c. Undefined
    d. Undefined

68. _____ is an accounting term which is commonly used in business.
    a. Thing
    b. Net profit0
    c. Undefined
    d. Undefined

69. _____, from Latin meaning "to make progress", is defined in two different ways. Pure economic _____ is the increase in wealth that an investor has from making an investment, taking into consideration all costs associated with that investment including the opportunity cost of capital.
    a. Profit0
    b. Thing
    c. Undefined
    d. Undefined

70. In mathematics, a _____ is the result of multiplying, or an expression that identifies factors to be multiplied.
    a. Thing
    b. Product0
    c. Undefined
    d. Undefined

71. In mathematics, factorization (British English: factorisation) or factoring is the decomposition of an object (for example, a number, a polynomial, or a matrix) into a product of other objects, or _____, which when multiplied together give the original.
    a. Thing
    b. Factors0
    c. Undefined
    d. Undefined

72. _____ is a physical property of a system that underlies the common notions of hot and cold; something that is hotter has the greater _____.
    a. Thing
    b. Temperature0
    c. Undefined
    d. Undefined

73. _____ are objects, characters, or other concrete representations of ideas, concepts, or other abstractions.
    a. Thing
    b. Symbols0
    c. Undefined
    d. Undefined

74. _____, either of the curved-bracket punctuation marks that together make a set of _____
    a. Thing
    b. Parentheses0
    c. Undefined
    d. Undefined

75. The _____ (symbol _____) and the millibar (symbol mbar, also mb) are units of pressure.
    a. Bar0
    b. Thing
    c. Undefined
    d. Undefined

76. _____ has many meanings, most of which simply .
    a. Thing
    b. Power0
    c. Undefined
    d. Undefined

Chapter 1. Real Numbers, Solving Equations, and Exponents

77. The word _____ comes from the Latin word linearis, which means created by lines.
    a. Linear0
    b. Thing
    c. Undefined
    d. Undefined

78. In mathematics and the mathematical sciences, a _____ is a fixed, but possibly unspecified, value. This is in contrast to a variable, which is not fixed.
    a. Constant0
    b. Thing
    c. Undefined
    d. Undefined

79. _____ is a fixed, but possibly unspecified, value. This is in contrast to a variable, which is not fixed.
    a. Thing
    b. Constant term0
    c. Undefined
    d. Undefined

80. In mathematics, a _____ is a constant multiplicative factor of a certain object. The object can be such things as a variable, a vector, a function, etc. For example, the _____ of $9x^2$ is 9.
    a. Thing
    b. Coefficient0
    c. Undefined
    d. Undefined

81. Equivalence is the condition of being _____ or essentially equal.
    a. Thing
    b. Equivalent0
    c. Undefined
    d. Undefined

82. In abstract algebra, _____ consists of sets with binary operations that satisfy certain axioms.
    a. Grouping0
    b. Thing
    c. Undefined
    d. Undefined

83. Two mathematical objects are equal if and only if they are precisely the same in every way. This defines a binary relation, _____, denoted by the sign of _____ "=" in such a way that the statement "x = y" means that x and y are equal.
    a. Equality0
    b. Thing
    c. Undefined
    d. Undefined

84. A _____ is a negotiable instrument instructing a financial institution to pay a specific amount of a specific currency from a specific demand account held in the maker/depositor's name with that institution. Both the maker and payee may be natural persons or legal entities.
    a. Thing
    b. Check0
    c. Undefined
    d. Undefined

85. In logic, a _____ consists of a logical incompatibility between two or more propositions.
    a. Thing
    b. Contradictions0
    c. Undefined
    d. Undefined

86. The material _____, also known as the material implication or truth functional _____, expresses a property of certain conditionals in logic.

a. Conditional0
b. Thing
c. Undefined
d. Undefined

87. In mathematics, a set is called _____ if there is a bijection between the set and some set of the form {1, 2, ..., n} where n is a natural number.
   a. Finite0
   b. Thing
   c. Undefined
   d. Undefined

88. A _____ is an equation in which each term is either a constant or the product of a constant times the first power of a variable.
   a. Linear equation0
   b. Thing
   c. Undefined
   d. Undefined

89. _____ is the estimation of a physical quantity such as distance, energy, temperature, or time.
   a. Thing
   b. Measurement0
   c. Undefined
   d. Undefined

90. _____, Greek for "knowledge of nature," is the branch of science concerned with the discovery and characterization of universal laws which govern matter, energy, space, and time.
   a. Thing
   b. Physics0
   c. Undefined
   d. Undefined

91. A _____ is a special kind of ratio, indicating a relationship between two measurements with different units, such as miles to gallons or cents to pounds.
   a. Rate0
   b. Thing
   c. Undefined
   d. Undefined

92. _____ is the fee paid on borrowed money.
   a. Thing
   b. Interest0
   c. Undefined
   d. Undefined

93. A _____ is one of the basic shapes of geometry: a polygon with three vertices and three sides which are straight line segments.
   a. Thing
   b. Triangle0
   c. Undefined
   d. Undefined

94. In mathematics, a _____ is the end result of a division problem. It can also be expressed as the number of times the divisor divides into the dividend.
   a. Quotient0
   b. Thing
   c. Undefined
   d. Undefined

95. _____ is a temperature scale named after the German physicist Daniel Gabriel _____ , who proposed it in 1724.
   a. Fahrenheit0
   b. Thing
   c. Undefined
   d. Undefined

Chapter 1. Real Numbers, Solving Equations, and Exponents

96. An _____ is a score derived from one of several different standardized tests attempting to measure intelligence.
    a. Thing
    b. Intelligence Quotient0
    c. Undefined
    d. Undefined

97. A _____ is a function that assigns a number to subsets of a given set.
    a. Measure0
    b. Thing
    c. Undefined
    d. Undefined

98. _____ is, or relates to, the _____ temperature scale .
    a. Celsius0
    b. Thing
    c. Undefined
    d. Undefined

99. In mathematics, there are several meanings of _____ depending on the subject.
    a. Thing
    b. Degree0
    c. Undefined
    d. Undefined

100. Acid _____ ratio measures the ability of a company to use its near cash or quick assets to immediately extinguish its current liabilities.
    a. Thing
    b. Test0
    c. Undefined
    d. Undefined

101. _____ is the distance around a given two-dimensional object. As a general rule, the _____ of a polygon can always be calculated by adding all the length of the sides together. So, the formula for triangles is P = a + b + c, where a, b and c stand for each side of it. For quadrilaterals the equation is P = a + b + c + d. For equilateral polygons, P = na, where n is the number of sides and a is the side length.
    a. Thing
    b. Perimeter0
    c. Undefined
    d. Undefined

102. _____ is a kind of property which exists as magnitude or multitude. It is among the basic classes of things along with quality, substance, change, and relation.
    a. Thing
    b. Amount0
    c. Undefined
    d. Undefined

103. _____ or investing is a term with several closely-related meanings in business management, finance and economics, related to saving or deferring consumption.
    a. Investment0
    b. Thing
    c. Undefined
    d. Undefined

104. The metre (or _____, see spelling differences) is a measure of length. It is the basic unit of length in the metric system and in the International System of Units (SI), used around the world for general and scientific purposes.
    a. Concept
    b. Meter0
    c. Undefined
    d. Undefined

105. A _____ is a four-sided plane figure that has two sets of opposite parallel sides.

a. Concept
b. Parallelogram0
c. Undefined
d. Undefined

106. A _____ is a quadrilateral, which is defined as a shape with four sides, which has a pair of parallel sides.
a. Thing
b. Trapezoid0
c. Undefined
d. Undefined

107. Deductive _____ is the kind of _____ in which the conclusion is necessitated by, or reached from, previously known facts (the premises).
a. Reasoning0
b. Thing
c. Undefined
d. Undefined

108. _____ was a Hungarian mathematician.
a. Person
b. George Polya0
c. Undefined
d. Undefined

109. A _____ is a simplified and structured visual representation of concepts, ideas, constructions, relations, statistical data, anatomy etc used in all aspects of human activities to visualize and clarify the topic.
a. Diagram0
b. Thing
c. Undefined
d. Undefined

110. _____ is a way of expressing a number as a fraction of 100 per cent meaning "per hundred".
a. Thing
b. Percent0
c. Undefined
d. Undefined

111. The plus and _____ signs are mathematical symbols used to represent the notions of positive and negative as well as the operations of addition and subtraction.
a. Minus0
b. Thing
c. Undefined
d. Undefined

112. A _____ is a unit of length, usually used to measure distance, in a number of different systems, including Imperial units, United States customary units and Norwegian/Swedish mil. Its size can vary from system to system, but in each is between 1 and 10 kilometers. In contemporary English contexts _____ refers to either:
a. Mile0
b. Thing
c. Undefined
d. Undefined

113. The payment of _____ as remuneration for services rendered or products sold is a common way to reward sales people.
a. Thing
b. Commission0
c. Undefined
d. Undefined

114. In mathematics, a _____ is an algebraic structure in which addition and multiplication are defined and have properties listed below.
a. Ring0
b. Thing
c. Undefined
d. Undefined

Chapter 1. Real Numbers, Solving Equations, and Exponents 13

115. A _____ is a type of debt. All material things can be lent but this article focuses exclusively on monetary loans. Like all debt instruments, a _____ entails the redistribution of financial assets over time, between the lender and the borrower.
 a. Thing
 b. Loan0
 c. Undefined
 d. Undefined

116. In mathematics, an _____, mean, or central tendency of a data set refers to a measure of the "middle" or "expected" value of the data set.
 a. Average0
 b. Concept
 c. Undefined
 d. Undefined

117. The _____, the average in everyday English, which is also called the arithmetic _____ (and is distinguished from the geometric _____ or harmonic _____). The average is also called the sample _____. The expected value of a random variable, which is also called the population _____.
 a. Thing
 b. Mean0
 c. Undefined
 d. Undefined

118. _____ is a form of periodic payment from an employer to an employee, which is specified in an employment contract.
 a. Gross pay0
 b. Thing
 c. Undefined
 d. Undefined

119. A _____ is a form of periodic payment from an employer to an employee, which is specified in an employment contract.
 a. Salary0
 b. Thing
 c. Undefined
 d. Undefined

120. In mathematics, a _____ is a two-dimensional manifold or surface that is perfectly flat.
 a. Plane0
 b. Thing
 c. Undefined
 d. Undefined

121. In mathematics, _____ are two-dimensional manifolds or surfaces that are perfectly flat.
 a. Thing
 b. Planes0
 c. Undefined
 d. Undefined

122. _____ is the transport of people on a trip/journey or the process or time involved in a person or object moving from one location to another.
 a. Travel0
 b. Thing
 c. Undefined
 d. Undefined

123. Regrouping is the act of putting ones into groups of 10. For example, the 1 on the far right of 131 would be denoted _____ if the digit of the number being subtracted is larger than 1, such as 131-99.
 a. Thing
 b. By 100
 c. Undefined
 d. Undefined

Chapter 1. Real Numbers, Solving Equations, and Exponents

124. A _____ is a landform that extends above the surrounding terrain in a limited area. A _____ is generally steeper than a hill, but there is no universally accepted standard definition for the height of a _____ or a hill although a _____ usually has an identifiable summit.
- a. Thing
- b. Mountain0
- c. Undefined
- d. Undefined

125. In botany, _____ are above-ground plant organs specialized for photosynthesis. Their characteristics are typically analyzed by using Fiobonacci's sequences.
- a. Leaves0
- b. Thing
- c. Undefined
- d. Undefined

126. U.S. liquid _____ is legally defined as 231 cubic inches, and is equal to 3.785411784 litres or abotu 0.13368 cubic feet. This is the most common definition of a _____. The U.S. fluid ounce is defined as 1/128 of a U.S. _____.
- a. Thing
- b. Gallon0
- c. Undefined
- d. Undefined

127. _____ is a set, with some particular properties and usually some additional structure, such as the operations of addition or multiplication, for instance.
- a. Thing
- b. Space0
- c. Undefined
- d. Undefined

128. _____ forms part of thinking. Considered the most complex of all intellectual functions, _____ has been defined as higher-order cognitive process that requires the modulation and control of more routine or fundamental skills.
- a. Problem solving0
- b. Thing
- c. Undefined
- d. Undefined

129. _____ is the state of being greater than any finite number, however large.
- a. Infinity0
- b. Thing
- c. Undefined
- d. Undefined

130. In mathematics, _____ expressions is used to reduce the expression into the lowest possible term.
- a. Thing
- b. Simplifying0
- c. Undefined
- d. Undefined

131. _____ is a notation for writing numbers that is often used by scientists and mathematicians to make it easier to write large and small numbers.
- a. Thing
- b. Scientific notation0
- c. Undefined
- d. Undefined

132. In combinatorial mathematics, a _____ is an un-ordered collection of unique elements.
- a. Concept
- b. Combination0
- c. Undefined
- d. Undefined

133. _____ is a method for differentiating expressions involving exponentiation the power operation.

a. Power rule0
b. Thing
c. Undefined
d. Undefined

134. A _____ is a numeral used to indicate a count. The most common use of the word today is to name the part of a fraction that tells the number or count of equal parts.
   a. Thing
   b. Numerator0
   c. Undefined
   d. Undefined

135. _____ is the scientific study of celestial objects such as stars, planets, comets, and galaxies; and phenomena that originate outside the Earth's atmosphere.
   a. Astronomy0
   b. Thing
   c. Undefined
   d. Undefined

136. The decimal separator is a symbol used to mark the boundary between the integral and the fractional parts of a decimal numeral. Terms implying the symbol used are _____ and decimal comma.
   a. Decimal point0
   b. Concept
   c. Undefined
   d. Undefined

137. _____ is electromagnetic radiation with a wavelength that is visible to the eye (visible _____) or, in a technical or scientific context, electromagnetic radiation of any wavelength.
   a. Light0
   b. Thing
   c. Undefined
   d. Undefined

138. The _____ or kilogramme is the SI base unit of mass. It is defined as being equal to the mass of the international prototype of the _____.
   a. Thing
   b. Kilogram0
   c. Undefined
   d. Undefined

139. In statistics, _____ means the most frequent value assumed by a random variable, or occurring in a sampling of a random variable.
   a. Mode0
   b. Concept
   c. Undefined
   d. Undefined

140. The _____ governs the differentiation of products of differentiable functions.
   a. Product rule0
   b. Thing
   c. Undefined
   d. Undefined

141. The _____ is a method of finding the derivative of a function that is the quotient of two other functions for which derivatives exist.
   a. Thing
   b. Quotient rule0
   c. Undefined
   d. Undefined

142. _____ are a measure of time.
   a. Minutes0
   b. Thing
   c. Undefined
   d. Undefined

143. In set theory and its applications throughout mathematics, _____ are a collection of sets (or sometimes other mathematical objects) that can be unambiguously defined by a property that all its members share.
   a. Classes0
   b. Thing
   c. Undefined
   d. Undefined

144. In mathematics, a _____ is a countable collection of open covers of a topological space that satisfies certain separation axioms.
   a. Thing
   b. Development0
   c. Undefined
   d. Undefined

145. _____ is often used to describe the measurement of the steepness, incline, gradient, or grade of a straight line. The _____ is defined as the ratio of the "rise" divided by the "run" between two points on a line, or in other words, the ratio of the altitude change to the horizontal distance between any two points on the line.
   a. Thing
   b. Slope0
   c. Undefined
   d. Undefined

146. In astronomy, geography, geometry and related sciences and contexts, a plane is said to be _____ at a given point if it is locally perpendicular to the gradient of the gravity field, i.e., with the direction of the gravitational force at that point.
   a. Thing
   b. Horizontal0
   c. Undefined
   d. Undefined

147. A _____ is a set of numbers that designate location in a given reference system, such as x,y in a planar _____ system or an x,y,z in a three-dimensional _____ system.
   a. Coordinate0
   b. Thing
   c. Undefined
   d. Undefined

148. In mathematics and its applications, a _____ is a system for assigning an n-tuple of numbers or scalars to each point in an n-dimensional space.
   a. Coordinate system0
   b. Concept
   c. Undefined
   d. Undefined

149. _____ means of or relating to the French philosopher and mathematician René Descartes.
   a. Thing
   b. Cartesian0
   c. Undefined
   d. Undefined

150. In mathematics, the _____ is used to determine each point uniquely in a plane through two numbers, usually called the x-coordinate and the y-coordinate of the point.
   a. Thing
   b. Cartesian coordinate system0
   c. Undefined
   d. Undefined

151. An _____ is a collection of two not necessarily distinct objects, one of which is distinguished as the first coordinate and the other as the second coordinate.
   a. Thing
   b. Ordered pair0
   c. Undefined
   d. Undefined

Chapter 1. Real Numbers, Solving Equations, and Exponents

152. _____ was a highly influential French philosopher, mathematician, scientist, and writer. Dubbed the "Founder of Modern Philosophy", and the "Father of Modern Mathematics". His theories provided the basis for the calculus of Newton and Leibniz, by applying infinitesimal calculus to the tangent line problem, thus permitting the evolution of that branch of modern mathematics

a. Person
b. Descartes0
c. Undefined
d. Undefined

153. In mathematics, the _____ of a coordinate system is the point where the axes of the system intersect.

a. Origin0
b. Thing
c. Undefined
d. Undefined

154. Any point where a graph makes contact with an coordinate axis is called an _____ of the graph

a. Intercept0
b. Thing
c. Undefined
d. Undefined

Chapter 2. Straight Lines and Functions

1. _____ is often used to describe the measurement of the steepness, incline, gradient, or grade of a straight line. The _____ is defined as the ratio of the "rise" divided by the "run" between two points on a line, or in other words, the ratio of the altitude change to the horizontal distance between any two points on the line.
   a. Slope0
   b. Thing
   c. Undefined
   d. Undefined

2. The _____ of measurement are a globally standardized and modernized form of the metric system.
   a. Units0
   b. Thing
   c. Undefined
   d. Undefined

3. In mathematics, defined and _____ are used to explain whether or not expressions have meaningful, sensible, and unambiguous values.
   a. Undefined0
   b. Thing
   c. Undefined
   d. Undefined

4. _____ is a notation for writing numbers that is often used by scientists and mathematicians to make it easier to write large and small numbers.
   a. Scientific notation0
   b. Thing
   c. Undefined
   d. Undefined

5. In astronomy, geography, geometry and related sciences and contexts, a plane is said to be _____ at a given point if it is locally perpendicular to the gradient of the gravity field, i.e., with the direction of the gravitational force at that point.
   a. Thing
   b. Horizontal0
   c. Undefined
   d. Undefined

6. Three or more points that lie on the same line are called _____.
   a. Collinear0
   b. Thing
   c. Undefined
   d. Undefined

7. The mathematical concept of a _____ expresses the intuitive idea of deterministic dependence between two quantities, one of which is viewed as primary and the other as secondary. A _____ then is a way to associate a unique output for each input of a specified type, for example, a real number or an element of a given set.
   a. Thing
   b. Function0
   c. Undefined
   d. Undefined

8. In geometry, two lines or planes if one falls on the other in such a way as to create congruent adjacent angles. The term may be used as a noun or adjective. Thus, referring to Figure 1, the line AB is the _____ to CD through the point B.
   a. Perpendicular0
   b. Thing
   c. Undefined
   d. Undefined

9. A _____ is a symbolic representation denoting a quantity or expression. It often represents an "unknown" quantity that has the potential to change.
   a. Variable0
   b. Thing
   c. Undefined
   d. Undefined

10. A _____ is a special kind of ratio, indicating a relationship between two measurements with different units, such as miles to gallons or cents to pounds.

Chapter 2. Straight Lines and Functions

a. Rate0
b. Thing
c. Undefined
d. Undefined

11. A _____ is a quantity that denotes the proportional amount or magnitude of one quantity relative to another.
   a. Ratio0
   b. Thing
   c. Undefined
   d. Undefined

12. In geometry, a line _____ is a part of a line that is bounded by two end points, and contains every point on the line between its end points.
   a. Segment0
   b. Concept
   c. Undefined
   d. Undefined

13. A _____ is a part of a line that is bounded by two end points, and contains every point on the line between its end points.
   a. Thing
   b. Line segment0
   c. Undefined
   d. Undefined

14. In mathematics, an _____, mean, or central tendency of a data set refers to a measure of the "middle" or "expected" value of the data set.
   a. Average0
   b. Concept
   c. Undefined
   d. Undefined

15. In mathematics, a _____ or rhodonea curve is a sinusoid plotted in polar coordinates.
   a. Thing
   b. Rose0
   c. Undefined
   d. Undefined

16. The word _____ comes from the Latin word linearis, which means created by lines.
   a. Thing
   b. Linear0
   c. Undefined
   d. Undefined

17. A _____ is an equation in which each term is either a constant or the product of a constant times the first power of a variable.
   a. Thing
   b. Linear equation0
   c. Undefined
   d. Undefined

18. In mathematics, the _____ of a coordinate system is the point where the axes of the system intersect.
   a. Thing
   b. Origin0
   c. Undefined
   d. Undefined

19. In geometry, a _____ is a special kind of point, usually a corner of a polygon, polyhedron, or higher dimensional polytope. In the geometry of curves a _____ is a point of where the first derivative of curvature is zero. In graph theory, a _____ is the fundamental unit out of which graphs are formed
   a. Vertex0
   b. Thing
   c. Undefined
   d. Undefined

20. In geometry, a _____ is defined as a quadrilateral where all four of its angles are right angles.

a. Thing
b. Rectangle0
c. Undefined
d. Undefined

21. A _____ is a four-sided plane figure that has two sets of opposite parallel sides.
    a. Concept
    b. Parallelogram0
    c. Undefined
    d. Undefined

22. In set theory and other branches of mathematics, the _____ of a collection of sets is the set that contains everything that belongs to any of the sets, but nothing else.
    a. Union0
    b. Thing
    c. Undefined
    d. Undefined

23. _____ is a mathematical science pertaining to the collection, analysis, interpretation or explanation, and presentation of data. It is applicable to a wide variety of academic disciplines, from the physical and social sciences to the humanities.
    a. Statistics0
    b. Thing
    c. Undefined
    d. Undefined

24. _____ are the basic objects of study in graph theory. Informally speaking, a graph is a set of objects called points, nodes, or vertices connected by links called lines or edges.
    a. Graphs0
    b. Thing
    c. Undefined
    d. Undefined

25. _____ is a test to determine if a relation or its graph is a function or not
    a. Vertical line test0
    b. Thing
    c. Undefined
    d. Undefined

26. Acid _____ ratio measures the ability of a company to use its near cash or quick assets to immediately extinguish its current liabilities.
    a. Thing
    b. Test0
    c. Undefined
    d. Undefined

27. In mathematics, a _____ may be described informally as a number that can be given by an infinite decimal representation.
    a. Thing
    b. Real number0
    c. Undefined
    d. Undefined

28. A _____ is a set of numbers that designate location in a given reference system, such as x,y in a planar _____ system or an x,y,z in a three-dimensional _____ system.
    a. Thing
    b. Coordinate0
    c. Undefined
    d. Undefined

29. In mathematics, a _____ of a k-place relation $L \subseteq X_1 \times \ldots \times X_k$ is one of the sets X_j, $1 \leq j \leq k$. In the special case where k = 2 and $L \subseteq X_1 \times X_2$ is a function $L : X_1 \to X_2$, it is conventional to refer to X_1 as the _____ of the function and to refer to X_2 as the codomain of the function.

a. Thing
b. Domain0
c. Undefined
d. Undefined

30. In mathematics, the _____ of a function is the set of all "output" values produced by that function. Given a function $f : A \to B$, the _____ of f, is defined to be the set $\{x \in B : x = f(a) \text{ for some } a \in A\}$.
   a. Range0
   b. Thing
   c. Undefined
   d. Undefined

31. An _____ or member of a set is an object that when collected together make up the set.
   a. Element0
   b. Thing
   c. Undefined
   d. Undefined

32. An _____ is a collection of two not necessarily distinct objects, one of which is distinguished as the first coordinate and the other as the second coordinate.
   a. Thing
   b. Ordered pair0
   c. Undefined
   d. Undefined

33. In mathematics, the conjugate _____ or adjoint matrix of an m-by-n matrix A with complex entries is the n-by-m matrix A* obtained from A by taking the transpose and then taking the complex conjugate of each entry.
   a. Thing
   b. Pairs0
   c. Undefined
   d. Undefined

34. An _____ is a straight line around which a geometric figure can be rotated.
   a. Thing
   b. Axis0
   c. Undefined
   d. Undefined

35. In elementary algebra, an _____ is a set that contains every real number between two indicated numbers and may contain the two numbers themselves.
   a. Interval0
   b. Thing
   c. Undefined
   d. Undefined

36. _____ is the fee paid on borrowed money.
   a. Interest0
   b. Thing
   c. Undefined
   d. Undefined

37. A _____ is a number that is less than zero.
   a. Negative number0
   b. Thing
   c. Undefined
   d. Undefined

38. In plane geometry, a _____ is a polygon with four equal sides, four right angles, and parallel opposite sides. In algebra, the _____ of a number is that number multiplied by itself.
   a. Square0
   b. Thing
   c. Undefined
   d. Undefined

39. In mathematics, a _____ of a number x is a number r such that $r^2 = x$, or in words, a number r whose square (the result of multiplying the number by itself) is x.

a. Square root0   b. Thing
c. Undefined   d. Undefined

40. In mathematics, a _____ of a complex-valued function f is a member x of the domain of f such that f(x) vanishes at x, that is, x : f (x) = 0.
   a. Thing
   b. Root0
   c. Undefined
   d. Undefined

41. A _____ is the part of a fraction that tells how many equal parts make up a whole, and which is used in the name of the fraction: "halves", "thirds", "fourths" or "quarters", "fifths" and so on.
   a. Concept
   b. Denominator0
   c. Undefined
   d. Undefined

42. _____ the expected value of a random variable displays the average or central value of the variable. It is a summary value of the distribution of the variable.
   a. Thing
   b. Determining0
   c. Undefined
   d. Undefined

43. An _____ is a combination of numbers, operators, grouping symbols and/or free variables and bound variables arranged in a meaningful way which can be evaluated..
   a. Expression0
   b. Thing
   c. Undefined
   d. Undefined

44. Mathematical _____ is used to represent ideas.
   a. Thing
   b. Notation0
   c. Undefined
   d. Undefined

45. _____ is used in mathematics, and throughout the physical sciences, engineering, and economics. The complexity of such notation ranges from relatively simple symbolic representations, such as numbers 1 and 2; function symbols sin and +, to conceptual symbols, such as lim and dy/dx; to equations and variables.
   a. Mathematical notation0
   b. Thing
   c. Undefined
   d. Undefined

46. The _____, the average in everyday English, which is also called the arithmetic _____ (and is distinguished from the geometric _____ or harmonic _____). The average is also called the sample _____. The expected value of a random variable, which is also called the population _____.
   a. Thing
   b. Mean0
   c. Undefined
   d. Undefined

47. A _____ is a first degree polynomial mathematical function of the form: f(x) = mx + b where m and b are real constants and x is a real variable.
   a. Thing
   b. Linear function0
   c. Undefined
   d. Undefined

48. A _____ is a deliberate process for transforming one or more inputs into one or more results.

Chapter 2. Straight Lines and Functions

a. Thing
b. Calculation0
c. Undefined
d. Undefined

49. In Euclidean geometry, a uniform _____ is a linear transformation that enlargers or diminishes objects, and whose _____ factor is the same in all directions. This is also called homothethy.
a. Thing
b. Scale0
c. Undefined
d. Undefined

50. In mathematics, the concept of a _____ tries to capture the intuitive idea of a geometrical one-dimensional and continuous object. A simple example is the circle.
a. Curve0
b. Thing
c. Undefined
d. Undefined

51. _____, either of the curved-bracket punctuation marks that together make a set of _____
a. Parentheses0
b. Thing
c. Undefined
d. Undefined

52. In linear algebra, the _____ of an n-by-n square matrix A is defined to be the sum of the elements on the main diagonal of A,
a. Trace0
b. Thing
c. Undefined
d. Undefined

53. In geographic information systems, a _____ comprises an entity with a geographic location, typically determined by points, arcs, or polygons. Carriageways and cadastres exemplify _____ data.
a. Thing
b. Feature0
c. Undefined
d. Undefined

54. In mathematics, the _____ of two sets A and B is the set that contains all elements of A that also belong to B (or equivalently, all elements of B that also belong to A), but no other elements.
a. Thing
b. Intersection0
c. Undefined
d. Undefined

55. In mathematics, an _____ is a statement about the relative size or order of two objects.
a. Thing
b. Inequality0
c. Undefined
d. Undefined

56. In mathematics, a _____ is a two-dimensional manifold or surface that is perfectly flat.
a. Plane0
b. Thing
c. Undefined
d. Undefined

57. A _____ is a set of possible values that a variable can take on in order to satisfy a given set of conditions, which may include equations and inequalities.
a. Solution set0
b. Thing
c. Undefined
d. Undefined

Chapter 2. Straight Lines and Functions

58. In mathematics, _____ geometry was the traditional name for the geometry of three-dimensional Euclidean space — for practical purposes the kind of space we live in.
   a. Thing
   b. Solid0
   c. Undefined
   d. Undefined

59. A _____ is a negotiable instrument instructing a financial institution to pay a specific amount of a specific currency from a specific demand account held in the maker/depositor's name with that institution. Both the maker and payee may be natural persons or legal entities.
   a. Thing
   b. Check0
   c. Undefined
   d. Undefined

60. In common philosophical language, a proposition or _____, is the content of an assertion, that is, it is true-or-false and defined by the meaning of a particular piece of language.
   a. Statement0
   b. Concept
   c. Undefined
   d. Undefined

61. _____ means of or relating to the French philosopher and mathematician René Descartes.
   a. Cartesian0
   b. Thing
   c. Undefined
   d. Undefined

62. In mathematics and its applications, a _____ is a system for assigning an n-tuple of numbers or scalars to each point in an n-dimensional space.
   a. Coordinate system0
   b. Concept
   c. Undefined
   d. Undefined

63. In mathematics, the _____ is used to determine each point uniquely in a plane through two numbers, usually called the x-coordinate and the y-coordinate of the point.
   a. Cartesian coordinate system0
   b. Thing
   c. Undefined
   d. Undefined

64. The word _____ is used in a variety of ways in mathematics.
   a. Index0
   b. Thing
   c. Undefined
   d. Undefined

65. The existence and properties of _____ are the basis of Euclid's parallel postulate. _____ are two lines on the same plane that do not intersect even assuming that lines extend to infinity in either direction.
   a. Parallel lines0
   b. Thing
   c. Undefined
   d. Undefined

66. In mathematics, the multiplicative inverse of a number x, denoted 1/x or x^{-1}, is the number which, when multiplied by x, yields 1. The multiplicative inverse of x is also called the _____ of x.
   a. Reciprocal0
   b. Thing
   c. Undefined
   d. Undefined

67. In arithmetic and algebra, when a number or expression is both preceded and followed by a binary operation, an _____ is required for which operation should be applied first.

Chapter 2. Straight Lines and Functions 25

   a. Order of operations0   b. Thing
   c. Undefined   d. Undefined

68. A _____ is a unit of length, usually used to measure distance, in a number of different systems, including Imperial units, United States customary units and Norwegian/Swedish mil. Its size can vary from system to system, but in each is between 1 and 10 kilometers. In contemporary English contexts _____ refers to either:
   a. Thing   b. Mile0
   c. Undefined   d. Undefined

69. _____ are a measure of time.
   a. Minutes0   b. Thing
   c. Undefined   d. Undefined

70. _____ is a branch of mathematics which deals with triangles, particularly triangles in a plane where one angle of the triangle is 90 degrees, and a variety of other topological relations such as spheres, in other branches, such as spherical _____.
   a. Trigonometry0   b. Thing
   c. Undefined   d. Undefined

71. _____ is a branch of mathematics concerning the study of structure, relation and quantity.
   a. Algebra0   b. Concept
   c. Undefined   d. Undefined

72. In mathematics, in the field of group theory, a _____ of a group is a quasisimple subnormal subgroup.
   a. Concept   b. Component0
   c. Undefined   d. Undefined

73. _____ is a mathematical operation, written a^n, involving two numbers, the base a and the exponent n.
   a. Thing   b. Exponentiating0
   c. Undefined   d. Undefined

74. _____ is a mathematical operation, written a^n, involving two numbers, the base a and the exponent n.
   a. Thing   b. Exponentiation0
   c. Undefined   d. Undefined

Chapter 3. Systems of Linear Equations

1. The word _____ comes from the Latin word linearis, which means created by lines.
   a. Linear0
   b. Thing
   c. Undefined
   d. Undefined

2. A _____ is an equation in which each term is either a constant or the product of a constant times the first power of a variable.
   a. Linear equation0
   b. Thing
   c. Undefined
   d. Undefined

3. In algebra, a _____ is a function depending on n that associates a scalar, det(A), to every $n \times n$ square matrix A.
   a. Determinant0
   b. Thing
   c. Undefined
   d. Undefined

4. Equivalence is the condition of being _____ or essentially equal.
   a. Thing
   b. Equivalent0
   c. Undefined
   d. Undefined

5. _____ is the property of two events happening at the same time in at least one reference frame.
   a. Thing
   b. Simultaneous0
   c. Undefined
   d. Undefined

6. _____ are a set of equations containing multiple variables.
   a. Thing
   b. Systems of equations0
   c. Undefined
   d. Undefined

7. _____ is the fee paid on borrowed money.
   a. Interest0
   b. Thing
   c. Undefined
   d. Undefined

8. Japanese mathematics, or _____ denotes a genuinely distinct kind of mathermatics developed in Japan duringthe Edo Period when the country was isolated from western influences
   a. Wasan0
   b. Thing
   c. Undefined
   d. Undefined

9. Mathematical _____ is used to represent ideas.
   a. Notation0
   b. Thing
   c. Undefined
   d. Undefined

10. Transport or _____ is the movement of people and goods from one place to another.
    a. Thing
    b. Transportation0
    c. Undefined
    d. Undefined

11. _____ is the interdisciplinary scientific study of the atmosphere that focuses on weather processes and forecasting.
    a. Meteorology0
    b. Thing
    c. Undefined
    d. Undefined

Chapter 3. Systems of Linear Equations

12. A _____ is a symbolic representation denoting a quantity or expression. It often represents an "unknown" quantity that has the potential to change.
    a. Thing
    b. Variable0
    c. Undefined
    d. Undefined

13. In mathematics, a _____ is a rectangular table of numbers or, more generally, a table consisting of abstract quantities that can be added and multiplied.
    a. Matrix0
    b. Thing
    c. Undefined
    d. Undefined

14. An _____ is a collection of two not necessarily distinct objects, one of which is distinguished as the first coordinate and the other as the second coordinate.
    a. Thing
    b. Ordered pair0
    c. Undefined
    d. Undefined

15. Initial objects are also called _____, and terminal objects are also called final.
    a. Thing
    b. Coterminal0
    c. Undefined
    d. Undefined

16. _____ is often used to describe the measurement of the steepness, incline, gradient, or grade of a straight line. The _____ is defined as the ratio of the "rise" divided by the "run" between two points on a line, or in other words, the ratio of the altitude change to the horizontal distance between any two points on the line.
    a. Slope0
    b. Thing
    c. Undefined
    d. Undefined

17. The act of _____ is the calculated approximation of a result which is usable even if input data may be incomplete, uncertain, or noisy.
    a. Thing
    b. Estimating0
    c. Undefined
    d. Undefined

18. The _____ are the only integral domain whose positive elements are well-ordered, and in which order is preserved by addition. Like the natural numbers, the _____ form a countably infinite set. The set of all _____ is usually denoted in mathematics by a boldface Z.
    a. Integers0
    b. Thing
    c. Undefined
    d. Undefined

19. In mathematics, the _____ of two sets A and B is the set that contains all elements of A that also belong to B (or equivalently, all elements of B that also belong to A), but no other elements.
    a. Thing
    b. Intersection0
    c. Undefined
    d. Undefined

20. A _____ is a negotiable instrument instructing a financial institution to pay a specific amount of a specific currency from a specific demand account held in the maker/depositor's name with that institution. Both the maker and payee may be natural persons or legal entities.

Chapter 3. Systems of Linear Equations

    a. Thing
    c. Undefined
    b. Check0
    d. Undefined

21. The _____ is used to discard one of the variables in an equation, only to replace it with the actual value when solving multiple equations.
    a. Substitution method0
    c. Undefined
    b. Thing
    d. Undefined

22. An _____ is a combination of numbers, operators, grouping symbols and/or free variables and bound variables arranged in a meaningful way which can be evaluated..
    a. Thing
    c. Undefined
    b. Expression0
    d. Undefined

23. _____ or arithmetics is the oldest and most elementary branch of mathematics, used by almost everyone, for tasks ranging from simple daily counting to advanced science and business calculations.
    a. Thing
    c. Undefined
    b. Arithmetic0
    d. Undefined

24. In mathematics, a _____ is a constant multiplicative factor of a certain object. The object can be such things as a variable, a vector, a function, etc. For example, the _____ of $9x^2$ is 9.
    a. Coefficient0
    c. Undefined
    b. Thing
    d. Undefined

25. In mathematics, the additive inverse, or _____ of a number n is the number that, when added to n, yields zero. The additive inverse of n is denoted −n. For example, 7 is −7, because 7 + (−7) = 0, and the additive inverse of −0.3 is 0.3, because −0.3 + 0.3 = 0.
    a. Thing
    c. Undefined
    b. Opposite0
    d. Undefined

26. In mathematics and the mathematical sciences, a _____ is a fixed, but possibly unspecified, value. This is in contrast to a variable, which is not fixed.
    a. Constant0
    c. Undefined
    b. Thing
    d. Undefined

27. In mathematics, the _____ of a number n is the number that, when added to n, yields zero. The _____ of n is denoted −n. For example, 7 is −7, because 7 + (−7) = 0, and the _____ of −0.3 is 0.3, because −0.3 + 0.3 = 0.
    a. Thing
    c. Undefined
    b. Additive inverse0
    d. Undefined

28. In linear algebra, the _____ of an n-by-n square matrix A is defined to be the sum of the elements on the main diagonal of A,
    a. Trace0
    c. Undefined
    b. Thing
    d. Undefined

29. In geographic information systems, a _____ comprises an entity with a geographic location, typically determined by points, arcs, or polygons. Carriageways and cadastres exemplify _____ data.

a. Thing	b. Feature0
c. Undefined	d. Undefined

30. A _____ is a type of debt. All material things can be lent but this article focuses exclusively on monetary loans. Like all debt instruments, a _____ entails the redistribution of financial assets over time, between the lender and the borrower.
a. Thing	b. Loan0
c. Undefined	d. Undefined

31. A _____ is a quantity that denotes the proportional amount or magnitude of one quantity relative to another.
a. Thing	b. Ratio0
c. Undefined	d. Undefined

32. A _____ is the result of the addition of a set of numbers. The numbers may be natural numbers, complex numbers, matrices, or still more complicated objects. An infinite _____ is a subtle procedure known as a series.
a. Thing	b. Sum0
c. Undefined	d. Undefined

33. The _____, the average in everyday English, which is also called the arithmetic _____ (and is distinguished from the geometric _____ or harmonic _____). The average is also called the sample _____. The expected value of a random variable, which is also called the population _____.
a. Mean0	b. Thing
c. Undefined	d. Undefined

34. A pair of angles is _____ if their respective measures sum to 180 degrees.
a. Supplementary0	b. Concept
c. Undefined	d. Undefined

35. A _____ is a function that assigns a number to subsets of a given set.
a. Thing	b. Measure0
c. Undefined	d. Undefined

36. A pair of angles are _____ if the sum of their angles is 90°.
a. Complementary0	b. Concept
c. Undefined	d. Undefined

37. In plane geometry, a _____ is a polygon with four equal sides, four right angles, and parallel opposite sides. In algebra, the _____ of a number is that number multiplied by itself.
a. Thing	b. Square0
c. Undefined	d. Undefined

38. Acid _____ ratio measures the ability of a company to use its near cash or quick assets to immediately extinguish its current liabilities.
a. Test0	b. Thing
c. Undefined	d. Undefined

Chapter 3. Systems of Linear Equations

39. _____ finance, in finance, a debt security, issued by Issuer
    a. Bond0
    b. Thing
    c. Undefined
    d. Undefined

40. _____ is a kind of property which exists as magnitude or multitude. It is among the basic classes of things along with quality, substance, change, and relation.
    a. Thing
    b. Amount0
    c. Undefined
    d. Undefined

41. A _____ is a fee added to a customer's bill.
    a. Service charge0
    b. Thing
    c. Undefined
    d. Undefined

42. The _____ of measurement are a globally standardized and modernized form of the metric system.
    a. Thing
    b. Units0
    c. Undefined
    d. Undefined

43. _____ is the application of tools and a processing medium to the transformation of raw materials into finished goods for sale.
    a. Thing
    b. Manufacturing0
    c. Undefined
    d. Undefined

44. A _____, sea mile or nautimile is a unit of length. It is accepted for use with the International System of Units (SI), but it is not an SI unit.[1] The _____ is used around the world for maritime and aviation purposes. It is commonly used in international law and treaties, especially regarding the limits of territorial waters. It developed from the geographical mile.
    a. Thing
    b. Nautical mile0
    c. Undefined
    d. Undefined

45. A _____ is a method for fastening or securing linear material such as rope by tying or interweaving. It may consist of a length of one or more segments of rope, string, webbing, twine, strap or even chain interwoven so as to create in the line the ability to bind to itself or to some other object - the "load". Knots have been the subject of interest both for their ancient origins, common use, and the mathematical implications of _____ theory.
    a. Thing
    b. Knot0
    c. Undefined
    d. Undefined

46. A _____ is a unit of length, usually used to measure distance, in a number of different systems, including Imperial units, United States customary units and Norwegian/Swedish mil. Its size can vary from system to system, but in each is between 1 and 10 kilometers. In contemporary English contexts _____ refers to either:
    a. Mile0
    b. Thing
    c. Undefined
    d. Undefined

47. _____ is a unit of speed, expressing the number of international miles covered per hour.
    a. Thing
    b. Miles per hour0
    c. Undefined
    d. Undefined

Chapter 3. Systems of Linear Equations

48. _____ is the transport of people on a trip/journey or the process or time involved in a person or object moving from one location to another.
    a. Thing
    b. Travel0
    c. Undefined
    d. Undefined

49. In mathematics, an _____, mean, or central tendency of a data set refers to a measure of the "middle" or "expected" value of the data set.
    a. Average0
    b. Concept
    c. Undefined
    d. Undefined

50. A _____ is one of the basic shapes of geometry: a polygon with three vertices and three sides which are straight line segments.
    a. Triangle0
    b. Thing
    c. Undefined
    d. Undefined

51. An _____ triange is a triangle with at least two sides of equal length.
    a. Thing
    b. Isosceles0
    c. Undefined
    d. Undefined

52. In mathematics, a _____ is an n-tuple with n being 3.
    a. Triple0
    b. Thing
    c. Undefined
    d. Undefined

53. One of the three formats applicable to a quadratic function is the _____ which is defined as $f = ax^2 + bx + c$.
    a. Thing
    b. General form0
    c. Undefined
    d. Undefined

54. _____ is the state of being greater than any finite real or natural number, however large.
    a. Thing
    b. Infinite0
    c. Undefined
    d. Undefined

55. In mathematics, a _____ is a two-dimensional manifold or surface that is perfectly flat.
    a. Plane0
    b. Thing
    c. Undefined
    d. Undefined

56. In mathematics, _____ are two-dimensional manifolds or surfaces that are perfectly flat.
    a. Thing
    b. Planes0
    c. Undefined
    d. Undefined

57. An _____ is one of eight divisions.
    a. Octant0
    b. Thing
    c. Undefined
    d. Undefined

58. _____ is a set, with some particular properties and usually some additional structure, such as the operations of addition or multiplication, for instance.

a. Space0
b. Thing
c. Undefined
d. Undefined

59. An _____ is when two lines intersect somewhere on a plane creating a right angle at intersection
a. Thing
b. Axes0
c. Undefined
d. Undefined

60. _____ are the basic objects of study in graph theory. Informally speaking, a graph is a set of objects called points, nodes, or vertices connected by links called lines or edges.
a. Graphs0
b. Thing
c. Undefined
d. Undefined

61. _____ usually refers to money in the form of liquid currency, such as banknotes or coins.
a. Cash0
b. Thing
c. Undefined
d. Undefined

62. The mathematical concept of a _____ expresses the intuitive idea of deterministic dependence between two quantities, one of which is viewed as primary and the other as secondary. A _____ then is a way to associate a unique output for each input of a specified type, for example, a real number or an element of a given set.
a. Thing
b. Function0
c. Undefined
d. Undefined

63. In chemistry, a _____ is substance made by combining two or more different materials in such a way that no chemical reaction occurs.
a. Mixture0
b. Thing
c. Undefined
d. Undefined

64. The Gaussian _____ is an algorithm which can be used to determine the solutions of a system of linear equations, to find the rank of a matrix, and to calculate the inverse of an invertible square matrix.
a. Thing
b. Elimination method0
c. Undefined
d. Undefined

65. _____ is an algorithm which can be used to determine the solutions of a system of linear equations, to find the rank of a matrix, and to calculate the inverse of an invertible square matrix.
a. Gaussian elimination0
b. Thing
c. Undefined
d. Undefined

66. In computer science an _____ is a data structure that consists of a group of elements having a single name that are accessed by indexing. In most programming languages each element has the same data type and the _____ occupies a continuous area of storage.
a. Array0
b. Thing
c. Undefined
d. Undefined

67. In mathematics, a matrix can be thought of as each row or _____ being a vector. Hence, a space formed by row vectors or _____ vectors are said to be a row space or a _____ space.

Chapter 3. Systems of Linear Equations

a. Column0
b. Concept
c. Undefined
d. Undefined

68. _____ are elementary linear transformations on a matrix which preserve matrix equivalence.
    a. Elementary row operations0
    b. Thing
    c. Undefined
    d. Undefined

69. _____ is a synonym for information.
    a. Data0
    b. Thing
    c. Undefined
    d. Undefined

70. Elementary _____ are simple transformations which can be applied to a matrix without changing the linear system of equations that it represents.
    a. Row operations0
    b. Thing
    c. Undefined
    d. Undefined

71. In mathematics, the _____ inverse of a number x, denoted 1/x or x^{-1}, is the number which, when multiplied by x, yields 1. The _____ inverse of x is also called the reciprocal of x.
    a. Multiplicative0
    b. Thing
    c. Undefined
    d. Undefined

72. In mathematics, a _____ may be described informally as a number that can be given by an infinite decimal representation.
    a. Thing
    b. Real number0
    c. Undefined
    d. Undefined

73. _____ element of an element x with respect to a binary operation * with identity element e is an element y such that x * y = y * x = e. In particular,
    a. Thing
    b. Inverse0
    c. Undefined
    d. Undefined

74. In linear algebra, the _____ refers to a matrix consisting of the coefficients of the variables in a set of linear equations.
    a. Coefficient matrix0
    b. Thing
    c. Undefined
    d. Undefined

75. In linear algebra, the _____ of a matrix is obtained by combining two matrices in such a way that a matrix of coefficients to which has been added a column of constants corresponds to the right hand side of the equations.
    a. Augmented matrix0
    b. Thing
    c. Undefined
    d. Undefined

76. _____ is a fixed, but possibly unspecified, value. This is in contrast to a variable, which is not fixed.
    a. Constant term0
    b. Thing
    c. Undefined
    d. Undefined

Chapter 3. Systems of Linear Equations

77. _____ is a term used to describe two matrices which can be transformed from one another using elementary row operations.
   a. Thing
   b. Row equivalent0
   c. Undefined
   d. Undefined

78. A _____ is a number, figure, or indicator that appears below the normal line of type, typically used in a formula, mathematical expression, or description of a chemical compound.
   a. Subscript0
   b. Thing
   c. Undefined
   d. Undefined

79. _____ is notation used to indicate some variable between two points each point being represented by one of the subscripts.
   a. Thing
   b. Double subscript notation0
   c. Undefined
   d. Undefined

80. In linear algebra, the _____ of a square matrix is the diagonal which runs from the top left corner to the bottom right corner.
   a. Main diagonal0
   b. Thing
   c. Undefined
   d. Undefined

81. A _____ can refer to a line joining two nonadjacent vertices of a polygon or polyhedron, or in some contexts any upward or downward sloping line. .
   a. Diagonal0
   b. Thing
   c. Undefined
   d. Undefined

82. Johann _____ was a German mathematician and scientist of profound genius who contributed significantly to many fields, including number theory, analysis, differential geometry, geodesy, magnetism, astronomy, and optics. He completed Disquisitiones Arithmeticae, his magnum opus, at the age of twenty-one.
   a. Person
   b. Carl Friedrich Gauss0
   c. Undefined
   d. Undefined

83. _____ is a special kind of square matrix where the entries below or above the main diagonal are zero.
   a. Thing
   b. Triangular form0
   c. Undefined
   d. Undefined

84. _____ or investing is a term with several closely-related meanings in business management, finance and economics, related to saving or deferring consumption.
   a. Investment0
   b. Thing
   c. Undefined
   d. Undefined

85. The easiest _____ prime numbers resides in the use of the Sieve of Eratosthenes, an algorithm that discovers all prime numbers to a specified integer.
   a. Method for finding0
   b. Thing
   c. Undefined
   d. Undefined

86. In linear algebra, a _____ of a matrix A is the determinant of some smaller square matrix, cut down from A.

Chapter 3. Systems of Linear Equations

a. Thing
b. Minor0
c. Undefined
d. Undefined

87. In mathematics, a _____ is the result of multiplying, or an expression that identifies factors to be multiplied.
a. Product0
b. Thing
c. Undefined
d. Undefined

88. An _____ of a product of sums expresses it as a sum of products by using the fact that multiplication distributes over addition.
a. Thing
b. Expansion0
c. Undefined
d. Undefined

89. A _____ is a numeral used to indicate a count. The most common use of the word today is to name the part of a fraction that tells the number or count of equal parts.
a. Thing
b. Numerator0
c. Undefined
d. Undefined

90. _____ is the distance around a given two-dimensional object. As a general rule, the _____ of a polygon can always be calculated by adding all the length of the sides together. So, the formula for triangles is P = a + b + c, where a, b and c stand for each side of it. For quadrilaterals the equation is P = a + b + c + d. For equilateral polygons, P = na, where n is the number of sides and a is the side length.
a. Thing
b. Perimeter0
c. Undefined
d. Undefined

91. The _____ (symbol _____) and the millibar (symbol mbar, also mb) are units of pressure.
a. Bar0
b. Thing
c. Undefined
d. Undefined

92. _____, from Latin meaning "to make progress", is defined in two different ways. Pure economic _____ is the increase in wealth that an investor has from making an investment, taking into consideration all costs associated with that investment including the opportunity cost of capital.
a. Thing
b. Profit0
c. Undefined
d. Undefined

93. In mathematics, an _____ is a statement about the relative size or order of two objects.
a. Thing
b. Inequality0
c. Undefined
d. Undefined

94. _____ is often described as a branch of applied mathematics and economics that studies situations where multiple players make decisions in an attempt to maximize their returns.
a. Thing
b. Game theory0
c. Undefined
d. Undefined

95. In mathematical analysis, _____ are objects which generalize functions and probability distributions.

Chapter 3. Systems of Linear Equations

a. Distribution0
b. Thing
c. Undefined
d. Undefined

96. A _____ is a set of possible values that a variable can take on in order to satisfy a given set of conditions, which may include equations and inequalities.
 a. Thing
 b. Solution set0
 c. Undefined
 d. Undefined

97. _____ are objects, characters, or other concrete representations of ideas, concepts, or other abstractions.
 a. Thing
 b. Symbols0
 c. Undefined
 d. Undefined

98. _____, verti-bar, vertical line, divider line, or pipe is the name of the character .
 a. Vertical bar0
 b. Thing
 c. Undefined
 d. Undefined

99. In geometry, a _____ is defined as a quadrilateral where all four of its angles are right angles.
 a. Rectangle0
 b. Thing
 c. Undefined
 d. Undefined

100. In arithmetic and algebra, when a number or expression is both preceded and followed by a binary operation, an _____ is required for which operation should be applied first.
 a. Order of operations0
 b. Thing
 c. Undefined
 d. Undefined

101. _____ is a mathematical operation, written a^n, involving two numbers, the base a and the exponent n.
 a. Exponentiating0
 b. Thing
 c. Undefined
 d. Undefined

102. _____ is a mathematical operation, written a^n, involving two numbers, the base a and the exponent n.
 a. Thing
 b. Exponentiation0
 c. Undefined
 d. Undefined

103. _____ is a notation for writing numbers that is often used by scientists and mathematicians to make it easier to write large and small numbers.
 a. Thing
 b. Scientific notation0
 c. Undefined
 d. Undefined

104. In mathematics, the _____ of a coordinate system is the point where the axes of the system intersect.
 a. Thing
 b. Origin0
 c. Undefined
 d. Undefined

105. In mathematics, the concept of a _____ tries to capture the intuitive idea of a geometrical one-dimensional and continuous object. A simple example is the circle.

Chapter 3. Systems of Linear Equations

a. Thing
b. Curve0
c. Undefined
d. Undefined

106. A _____ is a matrix form used when solving linear systems of equations.
a. Row echelon form0
b. Thing
c. Undefined
d. Undefined

107. In mathematics, a matrix is in row _____ if is satisfies the following requirements: • All nonzero rows are above any rows of all zeroes.   • The leading coefficient of a row is always strictly to the right of the leading coefficient of the row above it.
a. Thing
b. Echelon form0
c. Undefined
d. Undefined

Chapter 4. Polynomials

1. A _____ is a deliberate process for transforming one or more inputs into one or more results.
   a. Thing
   b. Calculation0
   c. Undefined
   d. Undefined

2. _____ is a branch of mathematics concerning the study of structure, relation and quantity.
   a. Concept
   b. Algebra0
   c. Undefined
   d. Undefined

3. _____ is a kind of property which exists as magnitude or multitude. It is among the basic classes of things along with quality, substance, change, and relation.
   a. Thing
   b. Amount0
   c. Undefined
   d. Undefined

4. There are two main approaches to _____ in mathematics. They are the model theory of _____ and the proof theory of _____.
   a. Thing
   b. Truth0
   c. Undefined
   d. Undefined

5. In mathematics, _____ is the decomposition of an object into a product of other objects, or factors, which when multiplied together give the original.
   a. Factoring0
   b. Thing
   c. Undefined
   d. Undefined

6. In mathematics, factorization (British English: factorisation) or factoring is the decomposition of an object (for example, a number, a polynomial, or a matrix) into a product of other objects, or _____, which when multiplied together give the original.
   a. Thing
   b. Factors0
   c. Undefined
   d. Undefined

7. In mathematics, a _____ is an expression that is constructed from one or more variables and constants, using only the operations of addition, subtraction, multiplication, and constant positive whole number exponents. is a _____. Note in particular that division by an expression containing a variable is not in general allowed in polynomials. [1]
   a. Thing
   b. Polynomial0
   c. Undefined
   d. Undefined

8. _____ the expected value of a random variable displays the average or central value of the variable.It is a summary value of the distribution of the variable.
   a. Thing
   b. Determining0
   c. Undefined
   d. Undefined

9. A _____ is a polynomial consisting of three terms; in other words, it is the sum of three monomials.
   a. Thing
   b. Trinomial0
   c. Undefined
   d. Undefined

10. In mathematics, a _____ is a particular kind of polynomial, having just one term.

Chapter 4. Polynomials

  a. Thing
  c. Undefined
  b. Monomial0
  d. Undefined

11. In elementary algebra, a _____ is a polynomial with two terms: the sum of two monomials. It is the simplest kind of polynomial except for a monomial.
  a. Binomial0
  b. Thing
  c. Undefined
  d. Undefined

12. A _____ is a symbolic representation denoting a quantity or expression. It often represents an "unknown" quantity that has the potential to change.
  a. Variable0
  b. Thing
  c. Undefined
  d. Undefined

13. In mathematics, a _____ can mean either an element of the set {1, 2, 3, ...} (i.e the positive integers) or an element of the set {0, 1, 2, 3, ...} (i.e. the non-negative integers).
  a. Concept
  b. Whole number0
  c. Undefined
  d. Undefined

14. _____ is a mathematical operation, written a^n, involving two numbers, the base a and the exponent n.
  a. Thing
  b. Exponentiating0
  c. Undefined
  d. Undefined

15. _____ is a mathematical operation, written a^n, involving two numbers, the base a and the exponent n.
  a. Thing
  b. Exponentiation0
  c. Undefined
  d. Undefined

16. A _____ is the part of a fraction that tells how many equal parts make up a whole, and which is used in the name of the fraction: "halves", "thirds", "fourths" or "quarters", "fifths" and so on.
  a. Concept
  b. Denominator0
  c. Undefined
  d. Undefined

17. In mathematics, a _____ is a constant multiplicative factor of a certain object. The object can be such things as a variable, a vector, a function, etc. For example, the _____ of $9x^2$ is 9.
  a. Coefficient0
  b. Thing
  c. Undefined
  d. Undefined

18. A _____ is the result of the addition of a set of numbers. The numbers may be natural numbers, complex numbers, matrices, or still more complicated objects. An infinite _____ is a subtle procedure known as a series.
  a. Thing
  b. Sum0
  c. Undefined
  d. Undefined

19. In mathematics, there are several meanings of _____ depending on the subject.
  a. Degree0
  b. Thing
  c. Undefined
  d. Undefined

Chapter 4. Polynomials

20. In mathematics and the mathematical sciences, a _____ is a fixed, but possibly unspecified, value. This is in contrast to a variable, which is not fixed.
    a. Constant0
    b. Thing
    c. Undefined
    d. Undefined

21. An _____ is a combination of numbers, operators, grouping symbols and/or free variables and bound variables arranged in a meaningful way which can be evaluated..
    a. Expression0
    b. Thing
    c. Undefined
    d. Undefined

22. A frame of _____ is a particular perspective from which the universe is observed.
    a. Thing
    b. Reference0
    c. Undefined
    d. Undefined

23. The word _____ comes from the Latin word linearis, which means created by lines.
    a. Linear0
    b. Thing
    c. Undefined
    d. Undefined

24. _____ has many meanings, most of which simply .
    a. Thing
    b. Power0
    c. Undefined
    d. Undefined

25. In mathematics, the additive inverse, or _____ of a number n is the number that, when added to n, yields zero. The additive inverse of n is denoted −n. For example, 7 is −7, because 7 + (−7) = 0, and the additive inverse of −0.3 is 0.3, because −0.3 + 0.3 = 0.
    a. Thing
    b. Opposite0
    c. Undefined
    d. Undefined

26. In astronomy, geography, geometry and related sciences and contexts, a plane is said to be _____ at a given point if it is locally perpendicular to the gradient of the gravity field, i.e., with the direction of the gravitational force at that point.
    a. Horizontal0
    b. Thing
    c. Undefined
    d. Undefined

27. In mathematics, _____ is an elementary arithmetic operation. When one of the numbers is a whole number, _____ is the repeated sum of the other number.
    a. Thing
    b. Multiplication0
    c. Undefined
    d. Undefined

28. Mathematical _____ is used to represent ideas.
    a. Notation0
    b. Thing
    c. Undefined
    d. Undefined

29. The _____, the average in everyday English, which is also called the arithmetic _____ (and is distinguished from the geometric _____ or harmonic _____). The average is also called the sample _____. The expected value of a random variable, which is also called the population _____.

a. Thing
b. Mean0
c. Undefined
d. Undefined

30. The mathematical concept of a _____ expresses the intuitive idea of deterministic dependence between two quantities, one of which is viewed as primary and the other as secondary. A _____ then is a way to associate a unique output for each input of a specified type, for example, a real number or an element of a given set.
a. Function0
b. Thing
c. Undefined
d. Undefined

31. Statistical _____ is a statistical procedure in which individual items are placed into groups based on quantitative information on one or more characteristics inherent in the items and based on a training set of previously labeled items.
a. Thing
b. Classification0
c. Undefined
d. Undefined

32. The _____ is the maximum of the degrees of all terms in the polynomial.
a. Thing
b. Degree of a polynomial0
c. Undefined
d. Undefined

33. In mathematics, and in particular in abstract algebra, the _____ is a property of binary operations that generalises the distributive law from elementary algebra.
a. Thing
b. Distributive property0
c. Undefined
d. Undefined

34. In mathematics, a _____ is the result of multiplying, or an expression that identifies factors to be multiplied.
a. Product0
b. Thing
c. Undefined
d. Undefined

35. _____ also sometimes known as the double distributive property or more colloquially as foiling, is commonly taught to US high school students learning algebra as a mnemonic for remembering how to multiply two binomials polynomials with two terms.
a. Thing
b. FOIL method0
c. Undefined
d. Undefined

36. The _____ is commonly taught to US high school students learning algebra as a mnemonic for remembering how to multiply two binomials.
a. FOIL rule0
b. Thing
c. Undefined
d. Undefined

37. A _____ is a three-dimensional solid object bounded by six square faces, facets, or sides, with three meeting at each vertex.
a. Thing
b. Cube0
c. Undefined
d. Undefined

38. _____ are of a number n in its third power-the result of multiplying it by itself three times.

a. Thing	b. Cubes0
c. Undefined	d. Undefined

39. In plane geometry, a _____ is a polygon with four equal sides, four right angles, and parallel opposite sides. In algebra, the _____ of a number is that number multiplied by itself.
 a. Square0	b. Thing
 c. Undefined	d. Undefined

40. The term _____ can refer to an integer which is the square of some other integer, or an algebraic expression that can be factored as the square of some other expression.
 a. Thing	b. Perfect square0
 c. Undefined	d. Undefined

41. In mathematics the _____ refers to the identity: $a^2 - b^2 = (a+b)(a-b)$
 a. Difference of two squares0	b. Thing
 c. Undefined	d. Undefined

42. A _____ is 360° or 2δ radians.
 a. Turn0	b. Thing
 c. Undefined	d. Undefined

43. _____ is the chance that something is likely to happen or be the case.
 a. Thing	b. Probability0
 c. Undefined	d. Undefined

44. _____ typically deals with the probability of several successive decisions, each of which has two possible outcomes.
 a. Binomial probability0	b. Thing
 c. Undefined	d. Undefined

45. _____ is the distance around a given two-dimensional object. As a general rule, the _____ of a polygon can always be calculated by adding all the length of the sides together. So, the formula for triangles is P = a + b + c, where a, b and c stand for each side of it. For quadrilaterals the equation is P = a + b + c + d. For equilateral polygons, P = na, where n is the number of sides and a is the side length.
 a. Thing	b. Perimeter0
 c. Undefined	d. Undefined

46. The metre (or _____, see spelling differences) is a measure of length. It is the basic unit of length in the metric system and in the International System of Units (SI), used around the world for general and scientific purposes.
 a. Meter0	b. Concept
 c. Undefined	d. Undefined

47. In geometry, a _____ is defined as a quadrilateral where all four of its angles are right angles.
 a. Thing	b. Rectangle0
 c. Undefined	d. Undefined

Chapter 4. Polynomials

48. _____ is electromagnetic radiation with a wavelength that is visible to the eye (visible _____) or, in a technical or scientific context, electromagnetic radiation of any wavelength.
    a. Light0
    b. Thing
    c. Undefined
    d. Undefined

49. In mathematics, _____ allows the rapid division of any polynomial by a binomial of the form x − r. It was described by Paolo Ruffini in 1809. _____ is a special case of long division when the divisor is a linear factor.
    a. Thing
    b. Ruffini's rule0
    c. Undefined
    d. Undefined

50. _____ is a payment made by a company to its shareholders
    a. Thing
    b. Dividend0
    c. Undefined
    d. Undefined

51. In mathematics, a _____ of an integer n, also called a factor of n, is an integer which evenly divides n without leaving a remainder.
    a. Thing
    b. Divisor0
    c. Undefined
    d. Undefined

52. In mathematics, a _____ may be described informally as a number that can be given by an infinite decimal representation.
    a. Thing
    b. Real number0
    c. Undefined
    d. Undefined

53. In arithmetic, _____ is a procedure for calculating the division of one integer, called the dividend, by another integer called the divisor, to produce a result called the quotient.
    a. Long division0
    b. Thing
    c. Undefined
    d. Undefined

54. In mathematics, computing, linguistics, and related disciplines, an _____ is a finite list of well-defined instructions for accomplishing some task which, given an initial state, will terminate in a defined end-state.
    a. Algorithm0
    b. Concept
    c. Undefined
    d. Undefined

55. The _____ is a theorem in mathematics which precisely expresses the outcome of the usual process of division of integers. The name is something of a misnomer, as it is a theorem, not an algorithm, i.e. a well-defined procedure for achieving a specific task — although the _____ can be used to find the greatest common divisor of two integers.
    a. Thing
    b. Division Algorithm0
    c. Undefined
    d. Undefined

56. A _____ is a numeral used to indicate a count. The most common use of the word today is to name the part of a fraction that tells the number or count of equal parts.
    a. Thing
    b. Numerator0
    c. Undefined
    d. Undefined

44 *Chapter 4. Polynomials*

57. In mathematics, a _____ is the end result of a division problem. It can also be expressed as the number of times the divisor divides into the dividend.
   a. Thing
   b. Quotient0
   c. Undefined
   d. Undefined

58. In mathematics, an inequality is a statement about the relative size or order of two objects. For example 14 > 10, or 14 is _____ 10.
   a. Greater than0
   b. Thing
   c. Undefined
   d. Undefined

59. A _____ is the sum of the elements of a sequence.
   a. Series0
   b. Thing
   c. Undefined
   d. Undefined

60. The _____ are the only integral domain whose positive elements are well-ordered, and in which order is preserved by addition. Like the natural numbers, the _____ form a countably infinite set. The set of all _____ is usually denoted in mathematics by a boldface Z .
   a. Thing
   b. Integers0
   c. Undefined
   d. Undefined

61. A _____ is the part of the dividend that is left over when the dividend is not evenly divisible by the divisor.
   a. Thing
   b. Remainder0
   c. Undefined
   d. Undefined

62. In mathematics, a _____ is an ordered list of objects. Like a set, it contains members, also called elements or terms, and the number of terms is called the length of the _____. Unlike a set, order matters, and the exact same elements can appear multiple times at different positions in the _____.
   a. Thing
   b. Sequence0
   c. Undefined
   d. Undefined

63. In mathematics, a subset of Euclidean space R^n is called _____ if it is closed and bounded.
   a. Thing
   b. Compact0
   c. Undefined
   d. Undefined

64. _____ in algebra is an application of polynomial long division.
   a. Remainder theorem0
   b. Thing
   c. Undefined
   d. Undefined

65. In mathematics, a _____ is a statement that can be proved on the basis of explicitly stated or previously agreed assumptions.
   a. Theorem0
   b. Thing
   c. Undefined
   d. Undefined

66. In mathematics, a _____ is a demonstration that, assuming certain axioms, some statement is necessarily true.

Chapter 4. Polynomials

    a. Thing
    b. Proof0
    c. Undefined
    d. Undefined

67. In mathematics, the _____ divisor of two non-zero integers, is the largest positive integer that divides both numbers without remainder.
    a. Thing
    b. Greatest common0
    c. Undefined
    d. Undefined

68. In Math the greates common divisor sometimes known as the _____ of two non- zero integers.
    a. Greatest common factor0
    b. Thing
    c. Undefined
    d. Undefined

69. _____ is the largest positive integer that divides both numbers without remainder.
    a. Thing
    b. Common Factor0
    c. Undefined
    d. Undefined

70. In mathematics, a _____ number (or a _____) is a natural number that has exactly two (distinct) natural number divisors, which are 1 and the _____ number itself.
    a. Thing
    b. Prime0
    c. Undefined
    d. Undefined

71. In abstract algebra, _____ consists of sets with binary operations that satisfy certain axioms.
    a. Grouping0
    b. Thing
    c. Undefined
    d. Undefined

72. In mathematics, the conjugate _____ or adjoint matrix of an m-by-n matrix A with complex entries is the n-by-m matrix A* obtained from A by taking the transpose and then taking the complex conjugate of each entry.
    a. Pairs0
    b. Thing
    c. Undefined
    d. Undefined

73. _____, either of the curved-bracket punctuation marks that together make a set of _____
    a. Thing
    b. Parentheses0
    c. Undefined
    d. Undefined

74. The _____ of measurement are a globally standardized and modernized form of the metric system.
    a. Thing
    b. Units0
    c. Undefined
    d. Undefined

75. The _____ of a solid object is the three-dimensional concept of how much space it occupies, often quantified numerically.
    a. Thing
    b. Volume0
    c. Undefined
    d. Undefined

76. A _____ is one of the basic shapes of geometry: a polygon with three vertices and three sides which are straight line segments.

Chapter 4. Polynomials

    a. Thing
    c. Undefined
    b. Triangle0
    d. Undefined

77. In mathematics, the _____ of a number n is the number that, when added to n, yields zero. The _____ of n is denoted −n. For example, 7 is −7, because 7 + (−7) = 0, and the _____ of −0.3 is 0.3, because −0.3 + 0.3 = 0.
    a. Additive inverse0
    c. Undefined
    b. Thing
    d. Undefined

78. _____ is a branch of mathematics which deals with triangles, particularly triangles in a plane where one angle of the triangle is 90 degrees, and a variety of other topological relations such as spheres, in other branches, such as spherical _____.
    a. Thing
    c. Undefined
    b. Trigonometry0
    d. Undefined

79. _____ is a mathematical subject that includes the study of limits, derivatives, integrals, and power series and constitutes a major part of modern university curriculum.
    a. Thing
    c. Undefined
    b. Calculus0
    d. Undefined

80. _____ is the fee paid on borrowed money.
    a. Interest0
    c. Undefined
    b. Thing
    d. Undefined

81. _____ interest refers to the fact that whenever interest is calculated, it is based not only on the original principal, but also on any unpaid interest that has been added to the principal.
    a. Compound0
    c. Undefined
    b. Thing
    d. Undefined

82. _____ refers to the fact that whenever interest is calculated, it is based not only on the original principal, but also on any unpaid interest that has been added to the principal. The more frequently interest is compounded, the faster the balance grows.
    a. Compound interest0
    c. Undefined
    b. Concept
    d. Undefined

83. A _____ is a special kind of ratio, indicating a relationship between two measurements with different units, such as miles to gallons or cents to pounds.
    a. Rate0
    c. Undefined
    b. Thing
    d. Undefined

84. In logic, a _____ consists of a logical incompatibility between two or more propositions.
    a. Contradictions0
    c. Undefined
    b. Thing
    d. Undefined

85. An _____ is an equality that remains true regardless of the values of any variables that appear within it, to distinguish it from an equality which is true under more particular conditions.

Chapter 4. Polynomials

a. Thing
b. Identity0
c. Undefined
d. Undefined

86. A _____ is an equation in which each term is either a constant or the product of a constant times the first power of a variable.
   a. Linear equation0
   b. Thing
   c. Undefined
   d. Undefined

87. In mathematics, a _____ is a polynomial equation of the second degree. The general form is $ax^2 + bx + c = 0$.
   a. Thing
   b. Quadratic equation0
   c. Undefined
   d. Undefined

88. A _____ is a negotiable instrument instructing a financial institution to pay a specific amount of a specific currency from a specific demand account held in the maker/depositor's name with that institution. Both the maker and payee may be natural persons or legal entities.
   a. Check0
   b. Thing
   c. Undefined
   d. Undefined

89. In mathematics, a _____ of a complex-valued function f is a member x of the domain of f such that f(x) vanishes at x, that is, x : f (x) = 0.
   a. Root0
   b. Thing
   c. Undefined
   d. Undefined

90. _____ means in succession or back-to-back
   a. Consecutive0
   b. Thing
   c. Undefined
   d. Undefined

91. _____ is a relation in Euclidean geometry among the three sides of a right triangle.
   a. Thing
   b. Pythagorean Theorem0
   c. Undefined
   d. Undefined

92. _____ has one 90° internal angle a right angle.
   a. Thing
   b. Right triangle0
   c. Undefined
   d. Undefined

93. The _____ of a right triangle is the triangle's longest side; the side opposite the right angle.
   a. Thing
   b. Hypotenuse0
   c. Undefined
   d. Undefined

94. A _____ is a function that assigns a number to subsets of a given set.
   a. Measure0
   b. Thing
   c. Undefined
   d. Undefined

95. In geometry and trigonometry, a _____ is defined as an angle between two straight intersecting lines of ninety degrees, or one-quarter of a circle.

48 *Chapter 4. Polynomials*

    a. Thing
    b. Right angle0
    c. Undefined
    d. Undefined

96. _____ was an Greek philosopher. He is best known for a theorem in trigonometry that bears his name.
    a. Pythagoras0
    b. Person
    c. Undefined
    d. Undefined

97. A _____ is a simplified and structured visual representation of concepts, ideas, constructions, relations, statistical data, anatomy etc used in all aspects of human activities to visualize and clarify the topic.
    a. Diagram0
    b. Thing
    c. Undefined
    d. Undefined

98. A _____ is a landform that extends above the surrounding terrain in a limited area. A _____ is generally steeper than a hill, but there is no universally accepted standard definition for the height of a _____ or a hill although a _____ usually has an identifiable summit.
    a. Mountain0
    b. Thing
    c. Undefined
    d. Undefined

99. A _____ is a unit of length, usually used to measure distance, in a number of different systems, including Imperial units, United States customary units and Norwegian/Swedish mil. Its size can vary from system to system, but in each is between 1 and 10 kilometers. In contemporary English contexts _____ refers to either:
    a. Thing
    b. Mile0
    c. Undefined
    d. Undefined

100. A _____ can refer to a line joining two nonadjacent vertices of a polygon or polyhedron, or in some contexts any upward or downward sloping line. .
    a. Diagonal0
    b. Thing
    c. Undefined
    d. Undefined

101. The _____ is a theorem for finding out the factors of a polynomial.
    a. Thing
    b. Factor theorem0
    c. Undefined
    d. Undefined

102. In mathematics, the _____ of two sets A and B is the set that contains all elements of A that also belong to B (or equivalently, all elements of B that also belong to A), but no other elements.
    a. Thing
    b. Intersection0
    c. Undefined
    d. Undefined

103. In mathematics, an _____ is a statement about the relative size or order of two objects.
    a. Inequality0
    b. Thing
    c. Undefined
    d. Undefined

104. In mathematics, the _____ (or modulus) of a real number is its numerical value without regard to its sign.
    a. Absolute value0
    b. Thing
    c. Undefined
    d. Undefined

Chapter 4. Polynomials

105. A _____ function is a function for which, intuitively, small changes in the input result in small changes in the output.
   a. Continuous0
   b. Event
   c. Undefined
   d. Undefined

106. In elementary algebra, an _____ is a set that contains every real number between two indicated numbers and may contain the two numbers themselves.
   a. Interval0
   b. Thing
   c. Undefined
   d. Undefined

107. A _____ is a set of possible values that a variable can take on in order to satisfy a given set of conditions, which may include equations and inequalities.
   a. Thing
   b. Solution set0
   c. Undefined
   d. Undefined

108. _____ are the basic objects of study in graph theory. Informally speaking, a graph is a set of objects called points, nodes, or vertices connected by links called lines or edges.
   a. Graphs0
   b. Thing
   c. Undefined
   d. Undefined

109. In mathematics, the concept of a _____ tries to capture the intuitive idea of a geometrical one-dimensional and continuous object. A simple example is the circle.
   a. Curve0
   b. Thing
   c. Undefined
   d. Undefined

110. _____ is the notation in which permitted values for a variable are expressed as ranging over a certain interval; "5 < x < 9" is an example of the application of _____.
   a. Thing
   b. Interval notation0
   c. Undefined
   d. Undefined

111. In arithmetic and algebra, when a number or expression is both preceded and followed by a binary operation, an _____ is required for which operation should be applied first.
   a. Thing
   b. Order of operations0
   c. Undefined
   d. Undefined

112. A _____ is a one-dimensional picture in which the integers are shown as specially-marked points evenly spaced on a line.
   a. Number line0
   b. Thing
   c. Undefined
   d. Undefined

113. _____ is often used to describe the measurement of the steepness, incline, gradient, or grade of a straight line. The _____ is defined as the ratio of the "rise" divided by the "run" between two points on a line, or in other words, the ratio of the altitude change to the horizontal distance between any two points on the line.
   a. Slope0
   b. Thing
   c. Undefined
   d. Undefined

Chapter 4. Polynomials

114. _____ is a notation for writing numbers that is often used by scientists and mathematicians to make it easier to write large and small numbers.
   a. Scientific notation0
   b. Thing
   c. Undefined
   d. Undefined

115. In geometry, a line _____ is a part of a line that is bounded by two end points, and contains every point on the line between its end points.
   a. Segment0
   b. Concept
   c. Undefined
   d. Undefined

116. A _____ is a part of a line that is bounded by two end points, and contains every point on the line between its end points.
   a. Line segment0
   b. Thing
   c. Undefined
   d. Undefined

117. _____ is a test to determine if a relation or its graph is a function or not
   a. Thing
   b. Vertical line test0
   c. Undefined
   d. Undefined

118. Acid _____ ratio measures the ability of a company to use its near cash or quick assets to immediately extinguish its current liabilities.
   a. Test0
   b. Thing
   c. Undefined
   d. Undefined

119. In mathematics, the _____ of a function is the set of all "output" values produced by that function. Given a function $f : A \to B$, the _____ of f, is defined to be the set $\{x \in B : x = f(a) \text{ for some } a \in A\}$.
   a. Range0
   b. Thing
   c. Undefined
   d. Undefined

120. In mathematics, a _____ of a k-place relation $L \subseteq X_1 \times \ldots \times X_k$ is one of the sets X_j, $1 \leq j \leq k$. In the special case where $k = 2$ and $L \subseteq X_1 \times X_2$ is a function $L : X_1 \to X_2$, it is conventional to refer to X_1 as the _____ of the function and to refer to X_2 as the codomain of the function.
   a. Thing
   b. Domain0
   c. Undefined
   d. Undefined

Chapter 5. Rational Expressions

1. _____ is a special mathematical relationship between two quantities. Two quantities are called proportional if they vary in such a way that one of the quantities is a constant multiple of the other, or equivalently if they have a constant ratio.
   - a. Thing
   - b. Proportionality0
   - c. Undefined
   - d. Undefined

2. The system of _____ numerals was a numeral system used in ancient Egypt. It was a decimal system, often rounded off to the higher power, written in hieroglyphs.
   - a. Egyptian0
   - b. Thing
   - c. Undefined
   - d. Undefined

3. In geometry, the _____ of an object is a point in some sense in the middle of the object.
   - a. Thing
   - b. Center0
   - c. Undefined
   - d. Undefined

4. _____ is an adjective usually refering to being in the centre.
   - a. Thing
   - b. Central0
   - c. Undefined
   - d. Undefined

5. _____ was an Indian mathematician and astronomer.
   - a. Person
   - b. Brahmagupta0
   - c. Undefined
   - d. Undefined

6. In mathematics, science including computer science, linguistics and engineering, an _____ is, generally speaking, an independent variable or input to a function.
   - a. Argument0
   - b. Thing
   - c. Undefined
   - d. Undefined

7. The deductive-nomological model is a formalized view of scientific _____ in natural language.
   - a. Thing
   - b. Explanation0
   - c. Undefined
   - d. Undefined

8. _____ or arithmetics is the oldest and most elementary branch of mathematics, used by almost everyone, for tasks ranging from simple daily counting to advanced science and business calculations.
   - a. Arithmetic0
   - b. Thing
   - c. Undefined
   - d. Undefined

9. The _____, the average in everyday English, which is also called the arithmetic _____ (and is distinguished from the geometric _____ or harmonic _____). The average is also called the sample _____. The expected value of a random variable, which is also called the population _____.
   - a. Mean0
   - b. Thing
   - c. Undefined
   - d. Undefined

10. In mathematics, a _____ number is a number which can be expressed as a ratio of two integers. Non-integer _____ numbers (commonly called fractions) are usually written as the vulgar fraction a / b, where b is not zero.
    - a. Rational0
    - b. Thing
    - c. Undefined
    - d. Undefined

Chapter 5. Rational Expressions

11. An _____ is a combination of numbers, operators, grouping symbols and/or free variables and bound variables arranged in a meaningful way which can be evaluated..
    a. Expression0
    b. Thing
    c. Undefined
    d. Undefined

12. In mathematics, a _____ is an expression that is constructed from one or more variables and constants, using only the operations of addition, subtraction, multiplication, and constant positive whole number exponents. is a _____. Note in particular that division by an expression containing a variable is not in general allowed in polynomials. [1]
    a. Polynomial0
    b. Thing
    c. Undefined
    d. Undefined

13. A _____ is a numeral used to indicate a count. The most common use of the word today is to name the part of a fraction that tells the number or count of equal parts.
    a. Numerator0
    b. Thing
    c. Undefined
    d. Undefined

14. A _____ is the part of a fraction that tells how many equal parts make up a whole, and which is used in the name of the fraction: "halves", "thirds", "fourths" or "quarters", "fifths" and so on.
    a. Denominator0
    b. Concept
    c. Undefined
    d. Undefined

15. A _____ is a symbolic representation denoting a quantity or expression. It often represents an "unknown" quantity that has the potential to change.
    a. Variable0
    b. Thing
    c. Undefined
    d. Undefined

16. Mathematical _____ is used to represent ideas.
    a. Notation0
    b. Thing
    c. Undefined
    d. Undefined

17. In mathematics, a _____ may be described informally as a number that can be given by an infinite decimal representation.
    a. Thing
    b. Real number0
    c. Undefined
    d. Undefined

18. The mathematical concept of a _____ expresses the intuitive idea of deterministic dependence between two quantities, one of which is viewed as primary and the other as secondary. A _____ then is a way to associate a unique output for each input of a specified type, for example, a real number or an element of a given set.
    a. Thing
    b. Function0
    c. Undefined
    d. Undefined

19. In mathematics, _____ is an elementary arithmetic operation. When one of the numbers is a whole number, _____ is the repeated sum of the other number.
    a. Thing
    b. Multiplication0
    c. Undefined
    d. Undefined

Chapter 5. Rational Expressions

20. A _____ signifies a point or points of probability on a subject e.g., the _____ of creativity, which allows for the formation of rule or norm or law by interpretation of the phenomena events that can be created.
    a. Thing
    b. Principle0
    c. Undefined
    d. Undefined

21. The _____ are the only integral domain whose positive elements are well-ordered, and in which order is preserved by addition. Like the natural numbers, the _____ form a countably infinite set. The set of all _____ is usually denoted in mathematics by a boldface Z .
    a. Integers0
    b. Thing
    c. Undefined
    d. Undefined

22. A _____ is a three-dimensional solid object bounded by six square faces, facets, or sides, with three meeting at each vertex.
    a. Thing
    b. Cube0
    c. Undefined
    d. Undefined

23. _____ are of a number n in its third power-the result of multiplying it by itself three times.
    a. Thing
    b. Cubes0
    c. Undefined
    d. Undefined

24. _____ is the largest positive integer that divides both numbers without remainder.
    a. Common Factor0
    b. Thing
    c. Undefined
    d. Undefined

25. In mathematics, a _____ is the end result of a division problem. It can also be expressed as the number of times the divisor divides into the dividend.
    a. Quotient0
    b. Thing
    c. Undefined
    d. Undefined

26. In mathematics, the additive inverse, or _____ of a number n is the number that, when added to n, yields zero. The additive inverse of n is denoted −n. For example, 7 is −7, because 7 + (−7) = 0, and the additive inverse of −0.3 is 0.3, because −0.3 + 0.3 = 0.
    a. Thing
    b. Opposite0
    c. Undefined
    d. Undefined

27. In mathematics, the _____ of a number n is the number that, when added to n, yields zero. The _____ of n is denoted −n. For example, 7 is −7, because 7 + (−7) = 0, and the _____ of −0.3 is 0.3, because −0.3 + 0.3 = 0.
    a. Thing
    b. Additive inverse0
    c. Undefined
    d. Undefined

28. In mathematics, a _____ is a number which can be expressed as a ratio of two integers. Non-integer rational numbers (commonly called fractions) are usually written as the vulgar fraction a / b, where b is not zero.
    a. Rational Number0
    b. Concept
    c. Undefined
    d. Undefined

Chapter 5. Rational Expressions

29. In mathematics, the multiplicative inverse of a number x, denoted 1/x or x^{-1}, is the number which, when multiplied by x, yields 1. The multiplicative inverse of x is also called the _____ of x.
    a. Reciprocal0
    b. Thing
    c. Undefined
    d. Undefined

30. In mathematics, a _____ of an integer n, also called a factor of n, is an integer which evenly divides n without leaving a remainder.
    a. Divisor0
    b. Thing
    c. Undefined
    d. Undefined

31. _____ is a mathematical operation, written a^n, involving two numbers, the base a and the exponent n.
    a. Exponentiating0
    b. Thing
    c. Undefined
    d. Undefined

32. _____ is a mathematical operation, written a^n, involving two numbers, the base a and the exponent n.
    a. Thing
    b. Exponentiation0
    c. Undefined
    d. Undefined

33. In mathematics, a _____ is any function which can be written as the ratio of two polynomial functions.
    a. Rational function0
    b. Thing
    c. Undefined
    d. Undefined

34. _____, either of the curved-bracket punctuation marks that together make a set of _____
    a. Thing
    b. Parentheses0
    c. Undefined
    d. Undefined

35. The _____ of a positive integer are the prime numbers that divide into that integer exactly, without leaving a remainder. The process of finding these numbers is called integer factorization, or prime factorization.
    a. Prime factor0
    b. Thing
    c. Undefined
    d. Undefined

36. In mathematics, a _____ is the result of multiplying, or an expression that identifies factors to be multiplied.
    a. Thing
    b. Product0
    c. Undefined
    d. Undefined

37. In mathematics, a _____ number (or a _____) is a natural number that has exactly two (distinct) natural number divisors, which are 1 and the _____ number itself.
    a. Prime0
    b. Thing
    c. Undefined
    d. Undefined

38. In mathematics, _____ is the decomposition of an object into a product of other objects, or factors, which when multiplied together give the original.
    a. Thing
    b. Factoring0
    c. Undefined
    d. Undefined

Chapter 5. Rational Expressions

39. In mathematics, factorization (British English: factorisation) or factoring is the decomposition of an object (for example, a number, a polynomial, or a matrix) into a product of other objects, or _____, which when multiplied together give the original.
   a. Thing
   b. Factors0
   c. Undefined
   d. Undefined

40. _____ is a natural number that has exactly two distinct natural number divisors, which are 1 and the _____ itself.
   a. Prime number0
   b. Thing
   c. Undefined
   d. Undefined

41. A _____ of a number is the product of that number with any integer.
   a. Thing
   b. Multiple0
   c. Undefined
   d. Undefined

42. The _____ of two integers is the smallest positive integer that is a multiple of both intergers.
   a. Least common multiple0
   b. Thing
   c. Undefined
   d. Undefined

43. Equivalence is the condition of being _____ or essentially equal.
   a. Equivalent0
   b. Thing
   c. Undefined
   d. Undefined

44. In mathematics, _____ expressions is used to reduce the expression into the lowest possible term.
   a. Thing
   b. Simplifying0
   c. Undefined
   d. Undefined

45. A _____ is the result of the addition of a set of numbers. The numbers may be natural numbers, complex numbers, matrices, or still more complicated objects. An infinite _____ is a subtle procedure known as a series.
   a. Sum0
   b. Thing
   c. Undefined
   d. Undefined

46. In topology and related areas of mathematics a _____ or Moore-Smith sequence is a generalization of a sequence, intended to unify the various notions of limit and generalize them to arbitrary topological spaces.
   a. Net0
   b. Thing
   c. Undefined
   d. Undefined

47. A _____ is the sum of the elements of a sequence.
   a. Thing
   b. Series0
   c. Undefined
   d. Undefined

48. In mathematics, an _____ is a statement about the relative size or order of two objects.
   a. Thing
   b. Inequality0
   c. Undefined
   d. Undefined

Chapter 5. Rational Expressions

49. In mathematics, a _____ is a constant multiplicative factor of a certain object. The object can be such things as a variable, a vector, a function, etc. For example, the _____ of $9x^2$ is 9.
   a. Thing
   b. Coefficient0
   c. Undefined
   d. Undefined

50. In mathematics and the mathematical sciences, a _____ is a fixed, but possibly unspecified, value. This is in contrast to a variable, which is not fixed.
   a. Constant0
   b. Thing
   c. Undefined
   d. Undefined

51. In mathematics, and in particular in abstract algebra, the _____ is a property of binary operations that generalises the distributive law from elementary algebra.
   a. Thing
   b. Distributive property0
   c. Undefined
   d. Undefined

52. A _____ is a negotiable instrument instructing a financial institution to pay a specific amount of a specific currency from a specific demand account held in the maker/depositor's name with that institution. Both the maker and payee may be natural persons or legal entities.
   a. Thing
   b. Check0
   c. Undefined
   d. Undefined

53. A _____ is a set of possible values that a variable can take on in order to satisfy a given set of conditions, which may include equations and inequalities.
   a. Solution set0
   b. Thing
   c. Undefined
   d. Undefined

54. In mathematics and more specifically set theory, the _____ set is the unique set which contains no elements.
   a. Thing
   b. Empty0
   c. Undefined
   d. Undefined

55. In logic and mathematics, logical _____ is a logical relation that holds between a set T of formulas and a formula B when every model (or interpretation or valuation) of T is also a model of B.
   a. Concept
   b. Implication0
   c. Undefined
   d. Undefined

56. A _____ is one of the basic shapes of geometry: a polygon with three vertices and three sides which are straight line segments.
   a. Thing
   b. Triangle0
   c. Undefined
   d. Undefined

57. _____ (or proportionality) are two quantities that vary in such a way that one of the quatities is a constant multiple of the other, or equivalently if they have a constant ratio.
   a. Proportions0
   b. Thing
   c. Undefined
   d. Undefined

58. A _____ is a quantity that denotes the proportional amount or magnitude of one quantity relative to another.

a. Ratio0
b. Thing
c. Undefined
d. Undefined

59. In mathematics, two quantities are called _____ if they vary in such a way that one of the quantities is a constant multiple of the other, or equivalently if they have a constant ratio.
    a. Proportional0
    b. Thing
    c. Undefined
    d. Undefined

60. The word _____ comes from the Latin word linearis, which means created by lines.
    a. Thing
    b. Linear0
    c. Undefined
    d. Undefined

61. In elementary algebra, an _____ is a set that contains every real number between two indicated numbers and may contain the two numbers themselves.
    a. Interval0
    b. Thing
    c. Undefined
    d. Undefined

62. _____ is the notation in which permitted values for a variable are expressed as ranging over a certain interval; "5 < x < 9" is an example of the application of _____.
    a. Interval notation0
    b. Thing
    c. Undefined
    d. Undefined

63. Acid _____ ratio measures the ability of a company to use its near cash or quick assets to immediately extinguish its current liabilities.
    a. Thing
    b. Test0
    c. Undefined
    d. Undefined

64. In geometry, an _____ is a point at which a line segment or ray terminates.
    a. Thing
    b. Endpoint0
    c. Undefined
    d. Undefined

65. In Euclidean geometry, a _____ is the set of all points in a plane at a fixed distance, called the radius, from a given point, the center.
    a. Thing
    b. Circle0
    c. Undefined
    d. Undefined

66. In mathematics, _____ geometry was the traditional name for the geometry of three-dimensional Euclidean space — for practical purposes the kind of space we live in.
    a. Solid0
    b. Thing
    c. Undefined
    d. Undefined

67. _____ of an object is its speed in a particular direction.
    a. Velocity0
    b. Thing
    c. Undefined
    d. Undefined

Chapter 5. Rational Expressions

68. _____ is often used to describe the measurement of the steepness, incline, gradient, or grade of a straight line. The _____ is defined as the ratio of the "rise" divided by the "run" between two points on a line, or in other words, the ratio of the altitude change to the horizontal distance between any two points on the line.
- a. Slope0
- b. Thing
- c. Undefined
- d. Undefined

69. _____ is a mathematical science pertaining to the collection, analysis, interpretation or explanation, and presentation of data. It is applicable to a wide variety of academic disciplines, from the physical and social sciences to the humanities.
- a. Thing
- b. Statistics0
- c. Undefined
- d. Undefined

70. In mathematics, an _____, mean, or central tendency of a data set refers to a measure of the "middle" or "expected" value of the data set.
- a. Concept
- b. Average0
- c. Undefined
- d. Undefined

71. _____ is the fee paid on borrowed money.
- a. Thing
- b. Interest0
- c. Undefined
- d. Undefined

72. _____ interest refers to the fact that whenever interest is calculated, it is based not only on the original principal, but also on any unpaid interest that has been added to the principal.
- a. Thing
- b. Compound0
- c. Undefined
- d. Undefined

73. _____ refers to the fact that whenever interest is calculated, it is based not only on the original principal, but also on any unpaid interest that has been added to the principal. The more frequently interest is compounded, the faster the balance grows.
- a. Compound interest0
- b. Concept
- c. Undefined
- d. Undefined

74. A _____ is a simplified and structured visual representation of concepts, ideas, constructions, relations, statistical data, anatomy etc used in all aspects of human activities to visualize and clarify the topic.
- a. Diagram0
- b. Thing
- c. Undefined
- d. Undefined

75. A _____ is a unit of length, usually used to measure distance, in a number of different systems, including Imperial units, United States customary units and Norwegian/Swedish mil. Its size can vary from system to system, but in each is between 1 and 10 kilometers. In contemporary English contexts _____ refers to either:
- a. Thing
- b. Mile0
- c. Undefined
- d. Undefined

76. _____ is a unit of speed, expressing the number of international miles covered per hour.

Chapter 5. Rational Expressions

    a. Thing
    c. Undefined

    b. Miles per hour0
    d. Undefined

77. A _____ is a special kind of ratio, indicating a relationship between two measurements with different units, such as miles to gallons or cents to pounds.
    a. Rate0
    c. Undefined
    b. Thing
    d. Undefined

78. _____ is the transport of people on a trip/journey or the process or time involved in a person or object moving from one location to another.
    a. Travel0
    c. Undefined
    b. Thing
    d. Undefined

79. A _____ is the part of the dividend that is left over when the dividend is not evenly divisible by the divisor.
    a. Thing
    c. Undefined
    b. Remainder0
    d. Undefined

80. _____ is a form of periodic payment from an employer to an employee, which is specified in an employment contract.
    a. Gross pay0
    c. Undefined
    b. Thing
    d. Undefined

81. A _____ is a form of periodic payment from an employer to an employee, which is specified in an employment contract.
    a. Salary0
    c. Undefined
    b. Thing
    d. Undefined

82. In mathematics, a _____ is a two-dimensional manifold or surface that is perfectly flat.
    a. Thing
    c. Undefined
    b. Plane0
    d. Undefined

83. _____ are a measure of time.
    a. Thing
    c. Undefined
    b. Minutes0
    d. Undefined

84. In mathematics, an inequality is a statement about the relative size or order of two objects. For example 14 > 10, or 14 is _____ 10.
    a. Greater than0
    c. Undefined
    b. Thing
    d. Undefined

85. _____, in economics and political economy, are the distributions or payments awarded to the various suppliers of the factors of production.
    a. Returns0
    c. Undefined
    b. Thing
    d. Undefined

86. _____ is a term applied when talking about the movement of air from one place to the next.

a. Wind speed0
c. Undefined
b. Thing
d. Undefined

87. _____ means in succession or back-to-back
   a. Thing
   b. Consecutive0
   c. Undefined
   d. Undefined

88. _____ are flexible, elastic objects used to store mechanical energy.
   a. Springs0
   b. Thing
   c. Undefined
   d. Undefined

89. In classical geometry, a _____ of a circle or sphere is any line segment from its center to its boundary. By extension, the _____ of a circle or sphere is the length of any such segment. The _____ is half the diameter. In science and engineering the term _____ of curvature is commonly used as a synonym for _____.
   a. Thing
   b. Radius0
   c. Undefined
   d. Undefined

90. In plane geometry, a _____ is a polygon with four equal sides, four right angles, and parallel opposite sides. In algebra, the _____ of a number is that number multiplied by itself.
   a. Thing
   b. Square0
   c. Undefined
   d. Undefined

91. _____ is the weakest of the four fundamental forces of bature, as described by Issac Newton
   a. Gravitational force0
   b. Thing
   c. Undefined
   d. Undefined

92. In physics, _____ is an influence that may cause an object to accelerate. It may be experienced as a lift, a push, or a pull. The actual acceleration of the body is determined by the vector sum of all forces acting on it, known as net _____ or resultant _____.
   a. Thing
   b. Force0
   c. Undefined
   d. Undefined

93. _____ is a relationship among three or more variables in which each pair of variables varies directly or inversely.
   a. Joint variation0
   b. Thing
   c. Undefined
   d. Undefined

94. In mathematics and logic, a _____ proof is a way of showing the truth or falsehood of a given statement by a straightforward combination of established facts, usually existing lemmas and theorems, without making any further assumptions.
   a. Direct0
   b. Thing
   c. Undefined
   d. Undefined

95. _____ is the relationship between two variables, like a ratio in which the two quantities being compared are different units.

Chapter 5. Rational Expressions

    a. Direct variation0   b. Thing
    c. Undefined   d. Undefined

96. _____ is the estimation of a physical quantity such as distance, energy, temperature, or time.
    a. Measurement0   b. Thing
    c. Undefined   d. Undefined

97. The _____ of a solid object is the three-dimensional concept of how much space it occupies, often quantified numerically.
    a. Volume0   b. Thing
    c. Undefined   d. Undefined

98. The _____ is the distance around a closed curve. _____ is a kind of perimeter.
    a. Circumference0   b. Thing
    c. Undefined   d. Undefined

99. In geometry, a _____ (Greek words diairo = divide and metro = measure) of a circle is any straight line segment that passes through the centre and whose endpoints are on the circular boundary, or, in more modern usage, the length of such a line segment. When using the word in the more modern sense, one speaks of the _____ rather than a _____, because all diameters of a circle have the same length. This length is twice the radius. The _____ of a circle is also the longest chord that the circle has.
    a. Diameter0   b. Thing
    c. Undefined   d. Undefined

100. U.S. liquid _____ is legally defined as 231 cubic inches, and is equal to 3.785411784 litres or abotu 0.13368 cubic feet. This is the most common definition of a _____. The U.S. fluid ounce is defined as 1/128 of a U.S. _____.
    a. Gallon0   b. Thing
    c. Undefined   d. Undefined

101. _____ is the property of a physical object that quantifies the amount of matter and energy it is equivalent to.
    a. Thing   b. Mass0
    c. Undefined   d. Undefined

102. _____ element of an element x with respect to a binary operation * with identity element e is an element y such that x * y = y * x = e. In particular,
    a. Inverse0   b. Thing
    c. Undefined   d. Undefined

103. A _____ is a one-dimensional picture in which the integers are shown as specially-marked points evenly spaced on a line.
    a. Thing   b. Number line0
    c. Undefined   d. Undefined

104. _____ is a notation for writing numbers that is often used by scientists and mathematicians to make it easier to write large and small numbers.

Chapter 5. Rational Expressions

    a. Thing
    c. Undefined
    b. Scientific notation0
    d. Undefined

105. In mathematics, a _____ is a rectangular table of numbers or, more generally, a table consisting of abstract quantities that can be added and multiplied.
    a. Matrix0
    c. Undefined
    b. Thing
    d. Undefined

106. In mathematics, _____ allows the rapid division of any polynomial by a binomial of the form x − r. It was described by Paolo Ruffini in 1809. _____ is a special case of long division when the divisor is a linear factor.
    a. Ruffini's rule0
    c. Undefined
    b. Thing
    d. Undefined

107. _____ is a test to determine if a relation or its graph is a function or not
    a. Vertical line test0
    c. Undefined
    b. Thing
    d. Undefined

108. In mathematics, the _____ of a function is the set of all "output" values produced by that function. Given a function $f : A \rightarrow B$, the _____ of f, is defined to be the set $\{x \in B : x = f(a) \text{ for some } a \in A\}$.
    a. Thing
    c. Undefined
    b. Range0
    d. Undefined

109. In mathematics, a _____ of a k-place relation $L \subseteq X_1 \times \ldots \times X_k$ is one of the sets X_j, $1 \leq j \leq k$. In the special case where k = 2 and $L \subseteq X_1 \times X_2$ is a function $L : X_1 \rightarrow X_2$, it is conventional to refer to X_1 as the _____ of the function and to refer to X_2 as the codomain of the function.
    a. Domain0
    c. Undefined
    b. Thing
    d. Undefined

110. _____ has one 90° internal angle a right angle.
    a. Right triangle0
    c. Undefined
    b. Thing
    d. Undefined

Chapter 6. Roots, Radicals and Complex Numbers

1. In mathematics, a _____ is a demonstration that, assuming certain axioms, some statement is necessarily true.
   a. Thing
   b. Proof0
   c. Undefined
   d. Undefined

2. In mathematics, a _____ number is a number which can be expressed as a ratio of two integers. Non-integer _____ numbers (commonly called fractions) are usually written as the vulgar fraction a / b, where b is not zero.
   a. Rational0
   b. Thing
   c. Undefined
   d. Undefined

3. In mathematics, an _____ number is any real number that is not a rational number- that is, it is a number which cannot be expressed as a fraction m/n, where m and n are integers.
   a. Irrational0
   b. Thing
   c. Undefined
   d. Undefined

4. In mathematics, an _____ is any real number that is not a rational number ¡ª that is, it is a number which cannot be expressed as m/n, where m and n are integers.
   a. Thing
   b. Irrational number0
   c. Undefined
   d. Undefined

5. A _____ is the large number 10100, that is, the digit 1 followed by one hundred zeros.
   a. Thing
   b. Googol0
   c. Undefined
   d. Undefined

6. _____ is the largest positive integer that divides both numbers without remainder.
   a. Common Factor0
   b. Thing
   c. Undefined
   d. Undefined

7. In common philosophical language, a proposition or _____, is the content of an assertion, that is, it is true-or-false and defined by the meaning of a particular piece of language.
   a. Concept
   b. Statement0
   c. Undefined
   d. Undefined

8. _____ is the symbold used to indicate the nth root of a number
   a. Thing
   b. Radical0
   c. Undefined
   d. Undefined

9. In mathematics, _____ are used to indicate the square root of a number.
   a. Thing
   b. Radicals0
   c. Undefined
   d. Undefined

10. In mathematics, a _____ may be described informally as a number that can be given by an infinite decimal representation.
    a. Thing
    b. Real number0
    c. Undefined
    d. Undefined

11. _____ is a mathematical operation, written a^n, involving two numbers, the base a and the exponent n.

a. Thing
b. Exponentiating0
c. Undefined
d. Undefined

12. _____ is a mathematical operation, written a^n, involving two numbers, the base a and the exponent n.
   a. Thing
   b. Exponentiation0
   c. Undefined
   d. Undefined

13. An _____ is a combination of numbers, operators, grouping symbols and/or free variables and bound variables arranged in a meaningful way which can be evaluated..
   a. Thing
   b. Expression0
   c. Undefined
   d. Undefined

14. In mathematics, an _____ number is a complex number whose square is a negative real number. They were defined in 1572 by Rafael Bombelli.
   a. Imaginary0
   b. Thing
   c. Undefined
   d. Undefined

15. A _____ is a three-dimensional solid object bounded by six square faces, facets, or sides, with three meeting at each vertex.
   a. Thing
   b. Cube0
   c. Undefined
   d. Undefined

16. A _____ of a number is a number a such that $a^3 = x$.
   a. Cube root0
   b. Thing
   c. Undefined
   d. Undefined

17. In plane geometry, a _____ is a polygon with four equal sides, four right angles, and parallel opposite sides. In algebra, the _____ of a number is that number multiplied by itself.
   a. Thing
   b. Square0
   c. Undefined
   d. Undefined

18. In mathematics, a _____ of a number x is a number r such that $r^2 = x$, or in words, a number r whose square (the result of multiplying the number by itself) is x.
   a. Thing
   b. Square root0
   c. Undefined
   d. Undefined

19. In mathematics, a _____ of a complex-valued function f is a member x of the domain of f such that f(x) vanishes at x, that is, $x : f(x) = 0$.
   a. Thing
   b. Root0
   c. Undefined
   d. Undefined

20. A _____ is the part of a fraction that tells how many equal parts make up a whole, and which is used in the name of the fraction: "halves", "thirds", "fourths" or "quarters", "fifths" and so on.
   a. Concept
   b. Denominator0
   c. Undefined
   d. Undefined

Chapter 6. Roots, Radicals and Complex Numbers

21. An _____ of a number *a* is a number *b* such that $b^n=a$.
    a. Nth root
    b. Thing
    c. Undefined
    d. Undefined

22. The _____ is the number or expression underneath the radical sign.
    a. Thing
    b. Radicand
    c. Undefined
    d. Undefined

23. The _____ integers are all the integers from zero on upwards.
    a. Thing
    b. Nonnegative
    c. Undefined
    d. Undefined

24. A _____ is the result of the addition of a set of numbers. The numbers may be natural numbers, complex numbers, matrices, or still more complicated objects. An infinite _____ is a subtle procedure known as a series.
    a. Sum
    b. Thing
    c. Undefined
    d. Undefined

25. A _____ decimal is a decimal fraction which ends after a definite number of digits.
    a. Thing
    b. Terminating
    c. Undefined
    d. Undefined

26. _____ represent rational numbers whose fractions in lowest terms are of the form $k/(2^n 5^m)$.
    a. Thing
    b. Terminating Decimals
    c. Undefined
    d. Undefined

27. _____ is the state of being greater than any finite real or natural number, however large.
    a. Infinite
    b. Thing
    c. Undefined
    d. Undefined

28. In mathematics, _____ are any real number that is not a rational number ¡ª that is, it is a number which cannot be expressed as m/n, where m and n are integers.
    a. Thing
    b. Irrational numbers
    c. Undefined
    d. Undefined

29. In mathematics, _____ expressions is used to reduce the expression into the lowest possible term.
    a. Simplifying
    b. Thing
    c. Undefined
    d. Undefined

30. A _____ is a deliberate process for transforming one or more inputs into one or more results.
    a. Thing
    b. Calculation
    c. Undefined
    d. Undefined

31. The term _____ can refer to an integer which is the square of some other integer, or an algebraic expression that can be factored as the square of some other expression.

Chapter 6. Roots, Radicals and Complex Numbers

a. Thing
b. Perfect square0
c. Undefined
d. Undefined

32. The word _____ is used in a variety of ways in mathematics.
    a. Thing
    b. Index0
    c. Undefined
    d. Undefined

33. A _____ is a number which is the cube of an integer.
    a. Perfect cube0
    b. Thing
    c. Undefined
    d. Undefined

34. _____, or Rationalisation in mathematics is the process of removing a square root or imaginary number from the denominator of a fraction.
    a. Rationalizing0
    b. Thing
    c. Undefined
    d. Undefined

35. A _____ is a numeral used to indicate a count. The most common use of the word today is to name the part of a fraction that tells the number or count of equal parts.
    a. Numerator0
    b. Thing
    c. Undefined
    d. Undefined

36. _____ or arithmetics is the oldest and most elementary branch of mathematics, used by almost everyone, for tasks ranging from simple daily counting to advanced science and business calculations.
    a. Arithmetic0
    b. Thing
    c. Undefined
    d. Undefined

37. In mathematics, a _____ is a number in the form of a + bi where a and b are real numbers, and i is the imaginary unit, with the property i 2 = −1. The real number a is called the real part of the _____, and the real number b is the imaginary part.
    a. Thing
    b. Complex number0
    c. Undefined
    d. Undefined

38. A _____ is a symbolic representation denoting a quantity or expression. It often represents an "unknown" quantity that has the potential to change.
    a. Variable0
    b. Thing
    c. Undefined
    d. Undefined

39. In mathematics, an inequality is a statement about the relative size or order of two objects. For example 14 > 10, or 14 is _____ 10.
    a. Greater than0
    b. Thing
    c. Undefined
    d. Undefined

40. _____, either of the curved-bracket punctuation marks that together make a set of _____
    a. Thing
    b. Parentheses0
    c. Undefined
    d. Undefined

Chapter 6. Roots, Radicals and Complex Numbers

41. Mathematical _____ is used to represent ideas.
    a. Notation0
    c. Undefined
    b. Thing
    d. Undefined

42. A _____ given two distinct points A and B on the _____, is the set of points C on the line containing points A and B such that A is not strictly between C and B.
    a. Ray0
    c. Undefined
    b. Thing
    d. Undefined

43. Equivalence is the condition of being _____ or essentially equal.
    a. Equivalent0
    c. Undefined
    b. Thing
    d. Undefined

44. In mathematics, a _____ is a constant multiplicative factor of a certain object. The object can be such things as a variable, a vector, a function, etc. For example, the _____ of $9x^2$ is 9.
    a. Coefficient0
    c. Undefined
    b. Thing
    d. Undefined

45. In mathematics, _____ growth occurs when the growth rate of a function is always proportional to the function's current size.
    a. Exponential0
    c. Undefined
    b. Thing
    d. Undefined

46. _____ is a notation for writing numbers that is often used by scientists and mathematicians to make it easier to write large and small numbers.
    a. Scientific notation0
    c. Undefined
    b. Thing
    d. Undefined

47. In mathematics, the additive inverse, or _____ of a number n is the number that, when added to n, yields zero. The additive inverse of n is denoted −n. For example, 7 is −7, because 7 + (−7) = 0, and the additive inverse of −0.3 is 0.3, because −0.3 + 0.3 = 0.
    a. Opposite0
    c. Undefined
    b. Thing
    d. Undefined

48. In mathematics, the _____ of a number n is the number that, when added to n, yields zero. The _____ of n is denoted −n. For example, 7 is −7, because 7 + (−7) = 0, and the _____ of −0.3 is 0.3, because −0.3 + 0.3 = 0.
    a. Thing
    c. Undefined
    b. Additive inverse0
    d. Undefined

49. In mathematics, _____ is an elementary arithmetic operation. When one of the numbers is a whole number, _____ is the repeated sum of the other number.
    a. Multiplication0
    c. Undefined
    b. Thing
    d. Undefined

50. In mathematics, a _____ is the result of multiplying, or an expression that identifies factors to be multiplied.

Chapter 6. Roots, Radicals and Complex Numbers

    a. Product0   b. Thing
    c. Undefined   d. Undefined

51. In mathematics, a _____ is an expression that is constructed from one or more variables and constants, using only the operations of addition, subtraction, multiplication, and constant positive whole number exponents. is a _____. Note in particular that division by an expression containing a variable is not in general allowed in polynomials. [1]
    a. Thing   b. Polynomial0
    c. Undefined   d. Undefined

52. In elementary algebra, a _____ is a polynomial with two terms: the sum of two monomials. It is the simplest kind of polynomial except for a monomial.
    a. Binomial0   b. Thing
    c. Undefined   d. Undefined

53. In algebra, a _____ is a binomial formed by taking the opposite of the second term of a binomial.
    a. Thing   b. Conjugate0
    c. Undefined   d. Undefined

54. In mathematics the _____ refers to the identity: $a^2 - b^2 = (a+b)(a-b)$
    a. Difference of two squares0   b. Thing
    c. Undefined   d. Undefined

55. In arithmetic and algebra, when a number or expression is both preceded and followed by a binary operation, an _____ is required for which operation should be applied first.
    a. Order of operations0   b. Thing
    c. Undefined   d. Undefined

56. The _____ is a number often encountered when taking the ratios of distances in simple geometric figures. It is approximately 1.6180339887.
    a. Thing   b. Golden ratio0
    c. Undefined   d. Undefined

57. A _____ is a quantity that denotes the proportional amount or magnitude of one quantity relative to another.
    a. Thing   b. Ratio0
    c. Undefined   d. Undefined

58. In geometry, a _____ is defined as a quadrilateral where all four of its angles are right angles.
    a. Thing   b. Rectangle0
    c. Undefined   d. Undefined

59. _____ is a branch of mathematics concerning the study of structure, relation and quantity.
    a. Concept   b. Algebra0
    c. Undefined   d. Undefined

60. A _____ is a rectangle whose side lengths are in the golden ratio, 1:, that is, approximately 1:1.618.

Chapter 6. Roots, Radicals and Complex Numbers

a. Thing
b. Golden rectangle0
c. Undefined
d. Undefined

61. A _____ is a function that assigns a number to subsets of a given set.
a. Thing
b. Measure0
c. Undefined
d. Undefined

62. In mathematics, the _____ of a function is the set of all "output" values produced by that function. Given a function $f : A \to B$, the _____ of f, is defined to be the set $\{x \in B : x = f(a) \text{ for some } a \in A\}$.
a. Range0
b. Thing
c. Undefined
d. Undefined

63. The mathematical concept of a _____ expresses the intuitive idea of deterministic dependence between two quantities, one of which is viewed as primary and the other as secondary. A _____ then is a way to associate a unique output for each input of a specified type, for example, a real number or an element of a given set.
a. Function0
b. Thing
c. Undefined
d. Undefined

64. In mathematics, a _____ of a k-place relation $L \subseteq X_1 \times \ldots \times X_k$ is one of the sets X_j, $1 \leq j \leq k$. In the special case where k = 2 and $L \subseteq X_1 \times X_2$ is a function $L : X_1 \to X_2$, it is conventional to refer to X_1 as the _____ of the function and to refer to X_2 as the codomain of the function.
a. Domain0
b. Thing
c. Undefined
d. Undefined

65. A _____ is a set of numbers that designate location in a given reference system, such as x,y in a planar _____ system or an x,y,z in a three-dimensional _____ system.
a. Thing
b. Coordinate0
c. Undefined
d. Undefined

66. An _____ or member of a set is an object that when collected together make up the set.
a. Element0
b. Thing
c. Undefined
d. Undefined

67. An _____ is a collection of two not necessarily distinct objects, one of which is distinguished as the first coordinate and the other as the second coordinate.
a. Ordered pair0
b. Thing
c. Undefined
d. Undefined

68. In mathematics, the conjugate _____ or adjoint matrix of an m-by-n matrix A with complex entries is the n-by-m matrix A* obtained from A by taking the transpose and then taking the complex conjugate of each entry.
a. Thing
b. Pairs0
c. Undefined
d. Undefined

69. In mathematics, the concept of a _____ tries to capture the intuitive idea of a geometrical one-dimensional and continuous object. A simple example is the circle.

Chapter 6. Roots, Radicals and Complex Numbers

    a. Curve0   b. Thing
    c. Undefined   d. Undefined

70. In geographic information systems, a _____ comprises an entity with a geographic location, typically determined by points, arcs, or polygons. Carriageways and cadastres exemplify _____ data.
    a. Feature0   b. Thing
    c. Undefined   d. Undefined

71. In mathematics, the _____ of a complex number z, is the second element of the ordered pair of real numbers representing z, i.e. if z = (x,y), or equivalently, z = x + iy, then the _____ of z is y.
    a. Thing   b. Imaginary part0
    c. Undefined   d. Undefined

72. The word _____ comes from the Latin word linearis, which means created by lines.
    a. Thing   b. Linear0
    c. Undefined   d. Undefined

73. A _____ is an equation in which each term is either a constant or the product of a constant times the first power of a variable.
    a. Linear equation0   b. Thing
    c. Undefined   d. Undefined

74. A _____ is a number that is less than zero.
    a. Negative number0   b. Thing
    c. Undefined   d. Undefined

75. In mathematics, a _____ is a polynomial equation of the second degree. The general form is $ax^2 + bx + c = 0$.
    a. Thing   b. Quadratic equation0
    c. Undefined   d. Undefined

76. In mathematics, the _____ of a complex number z, is the first element of the ordered pair of real numbers representing z, i.e. if z = (x,y), or equivalently, z = x + iy, then the _____ of z is x. It is denoted by Re{z} . The complex function which maps z to the _____ of z is not holomorphic.
    a. Thing   b. Real part0
    c. Undefined   d. Undefined

77. In mathematics, an _____ is a complex number whose square is a negative real number. They were defined in 1572 by Rafael Bombelli.
    a. Thing   b. Imaginary number0
    c. Undefined   d. Undefined

78. In mathematics, a _____ can mean either an element of the set {1, 2, 3, ...} (i.e the positive integers) or an element of the set {0, 1, 2, 3, ...} (i.e. the non-negative integers).
    a. Whole number0   b. Concept
    c. Undefined   d. Undefined

Chapter 6. Roots, Radicals and Complex Numbers

79. _____ also sometimes known as the double distributive property or more colloquially as foiling, is commonly taught to US high school students learning algebra as a mnemonic for remembering how to multiply two binomials polynomials with two terms.
    a. Thing
    b. FOIL method0
    c. Undefined
    d. Undefined

80. The _____ is commonly taught to US high school students learning algebra as a mnemonic for remembering how to multiply two binomials.
    a. FOIL rule0
    b. Thing
    c. Undefined
    d. Undefined

81. _____ has many meanings, most of which simply .
    a. Power0
    b. Thing
    c. Undefined
    d. Undefined

82. A _____ of a number is the product of that number with any integer.
    a. Thing
    b. Multiple0
    c. Undefined
    d. Undefined

83. In mathematics, the _____ (or modulus) of a real number is its numerical value without regard to its sign.
    a. Absolute value0
    b. Thing
    c. Undefined
    d. Undefined

84. In mathematics, a _____ is the end result of a division problem. It can also be expressed as the number of times the divisor divides into the dividend.
    a. Thing
    b. Quotient0
    c. Undefined
    d. Undefined

85. The _____ is a method of finding the derivative of a function that is the quotient of two other functions for which derivatives exist.
    a. Quotient rule0
    b. Thing
    c. Undefined
    d. Undefined

86. _____ is a method for differentiating expressions involving exponentiation the power operation.
    a. Thing
    b. Power rule0
    c. Undefined
    d. Undefined

87. Two mathematical objects are equal if and only if they are precisely the same in every way. This defines a binary relation, _____, denoted by the sign of _____ "=" in such a way that the statement "x = y" means that x and y are equal.
    a. Thing
    b. Equality0
    c. Undefined
    d. Undefined

88. Acid _____ ratio measures the ability of a company to use its near cash or quick assets to immediately extinguish its current liabilities.

Chapter 6. Roots, Radicals and Complex Numbers

   a. Test0
   c. Undefined
   b. Thing
   d. Undefined

89. A _____ is a one-dimensional picture in which the integers are shown as specially-marked points evenly spaced on a line.
   a. Number line0
   c. Undefined
   b. Thing
   d. Undefined

90. In mathematics, an _____ is a statement about the relative size or order of two objects.
   a. Inequality0
   c. Undefined
   b. Thing
   d. Undefined

91. The _____ of a solid object is the three-dimensional concept of how much space it occupies, often quantified numerically.
   a. Volume0
   c. Undefined
   b. Thing
   d. Undefined

92. In physics, _____ is an influence that may cause an object to accelerate. It may be experienced as a lift, a push, or a pull. The actual acceleration of the body is determined by the vector sum of all forces acting on it, known as net _____ or resultant _____.
   a. Thing
   c. Undefined
   b. Force0
   d. Undefined

93. In mathematics, two quantities are called _____ if they vary in such a way that one of the quantities is a constant multiple of the other, or equivalently if they have a constant ratio.
   a. Proportional0
   c. Undefined
   b. Thing
   d. Undefined

94. In geometry, a _____ (Greek words diairo = divide and metro = measure) of a circle is any straight line segment that passes through the centre and whose endpoints are on the circular boundary, or, in more modern usage, the length of such a line segment. When using the word in the more modern sense, one speaks of the _____ rather than a _____, because all diameters of a circle have the same length. This length is twice the radius. The _____ of a circle is also the longest chord that the circle has.
   a. Diameter0
   c. Undefined
   b. Thing
   d. Undefined

95. In mathematics, _____ is the decomposition of an object into a product of other objects, or factors, which when multiplied together give the original.
   a. Thing
   c. Undefined
   b. Factoring0
   d. Undefined

96. In mathematics, _____ allows the rapid division of any polynomial by a binomial of the form x − r. It was described by Paolo Ruffini in 1809. _____ is a special case of long division when the divisor is a linear factor.
   a. Thing
   c. Undefined
   b. Ruffini's rule0
   d. Undefined

Chapter 6. Roots, Radicals and Complex Numbers

97. _____ is a test to determine if a relation or its graph is a function or not
   a. Vertical line test0
   b. Thing
   c. Undefined
   d. Undefined

98. _____ are the basic objects of study in graph theory. Informally speaking, a graph is a set of objects called points, nodes, or vertices connected by links called lines or edges.
   a. Thing
   b. Graphs0
   c. Undefined
   d. Undefined

99. A _____ is a unit of length, usually used to measure distance, in a number of different systems, including Imperial units, United States customary units and Norwegian/Swedish mil. Its size can vary from system to system, but in each is between 1 and 10 kilometers. In contemporary English contexts _____ refers to either:
   a. Mile0
   b. Thing
   c. Undefined
   d. Undefined

100. _____ is the fee paid on borrowed money.
   a. Interest0
   b. Thing
   c. Undefined
   d. Undefined

101. In linear algebra, the _____ of an n-by-n square matrix A is defined to be the sum of the elements on the main diagonal of A,
   a. Thing
   b. Trace0
   c. Undefined
   d. Undefined

Chapter 7. Quadratic Equations

1. A quadratic equation with real solutions, called roots, which may be real or complex, is given by the _____: $x = \frac{-b \pm \sqrt{b^2 - 4ac}}{2a}$.
   a. Thing
   b. Quadratic formula0
   c. Undefined
   d. Undefined

2. In mathematics, a _____ is a constant multiplicative factor of a certain object. The object can be such things as a variable, a vector, a function, etc. For example, the _____ of $9x^2$ is 9.
   a. Thing
   b. Coefficient0
   c. Undefined
   d. Undefined

3. In mathematics, a _____ of a complex-valued function f is a member x of the domain of f such that f(x) vanishes at x, that is, $x : f(x) = 0$.
   a. Thing
   b. Root0
   c. Undefined
   d. Undefined

4. In mathematics, a _____ is a polynomial equation of the third degree.
   a. Cubic equation0
   b. Thing
   c. Undefined
   d. Undefined

5. In mathematics and elsewhere, the adjective _____ means fourth order, such as the function x4. A _____ number is a number which equals the fourth power of an integer.
   a. Thing
   b. Quartic0
   c. Undefined
   d. Undefined

6. The word _____ comes from the Latin word linearis, which means created by lines.
   a. Linear0
   b. Thing
   c. Undefined
   d. Undefined

7. In mathematics, a _____ is an expression that is constructed from one or more variables and constants, using only the operations of addition, subtraction, multiplication, and constant positive whole number exponents. is a _____. Note in particular that division by an expression containing a variable is not in general allowed in polynomials. [1]
   a. Thing
   b. Polynomial0
   c. Undefined
   d. Undefined

8. _____ is the symbol used to indicate the nth root of a number
   a. Radical0
   b. Thing
   c. Undefined
   d. Undefined

9. _____ was a French mathematician born in Bourg-la-Reine.
   a. Evariste Galois0
   b. Thing
   c. Undefined
   d. Undefined

10. Évariste _____ was a French mathematician born in Bourg-la-Reine.
    a. Person
    b. Galois0
    c. Undefined
    d. Undefined

11. _____ is a branch of mathematics concerning the study of structure, relation and quantity.

Chapter 7. Quadratic Equations

    a. Algebra0
    c. Undefined
    b. Concept
    d. Undefined

12. In mathematics, a _____ is a demonstration that, assuming certain axioms, some statement is necessarily true.
    a. Thing
    c. Undefined
    b. Proof0
    d. Undefined

13. _____ is that branch of mathematics concerned with the study of groups. These are sets with a rule, or operation. The operation in a group must satisfy closure and have these three additional properties: 1) The operation must have the property of associativity. 2) There must be an identity element. 3) Every element must have a corresponding inverse element. _____ is used throughout mathematics and has several applications in physics and chemistry. Groups can be finite or infinite. A classification of finite simple groups, completed in 1983, is one of the major achievements of mathematics in the 20th century.
    a. Thing
    c. Undefined
    b. Group theory0
    d. Undefined

14. Multiple Signal Classification, also known as _____, is an algorithm used for frequency estimation and emitter location.
    a. Music0
    c. Undefined
    b. Thing
    d. Undefined

15. In mathematics, a _____ is a polynomial equation of the second degree. The general form is $ax^2 + bx + c = 0$.
    a. Thing
    c. Undefined
    b. Quadratic equation0
    d. Undefined

16. _____ is the design, analysis, and/or construction of works for practical purposes.
    a. Thing
    c. Undefined
    b. Engineering0
    d. Undefined

17. _____ of a polynomial with real or complex coefficients is a certain expression in the coefficients of the polynomial which is equal to zero if and only if the polynomial has a multiple root i.e. a root with multiplicity greater than one in the complex numbers.
    a. Discriminant0
    c. Undefined
    b. Thing
    d. Undefined

18. In plane geometry, a _____ is a polygon with four equal sides, four right angles, and parallel opposite sides. In algebra, the _____ of a number is that number multiplied by itself.
    a. Thing
    c. Undefined
    b. Square0
    d. Undefined

19. In mathematics, a _____ of a number x is a number r such that $r^2 = x$, or in words, a number r whose square (the result of multiplying the number by itself) is x.
    a. Thing
    c. Undefined
    b. Square root0
    d. Undefined

Chapter 7. Quadratic Equations

20. _____ is a technique used in algebra to solve quadratic equations, in analytic geometry for determining the shapes of graphs, and in calculus for computing integrals, including, but hardly limited to, the integrals that define Laplace transforms. The essential objective is to reduce a quadratic polynomial in a variable in an equation or expression to a squared polynomial of linear order. This can reduce an equation or integral to one that is more easily solved or evaluated.
   a. Completing the square0
   b. Thing
   c. Undefined
   d. Undefined

21. In mathematics, _____ is the decomposition of an object into a product of other objects, or factors, which when multiplied together give the original.
   a. Factoring0
   b. Thing
   c. Undefined
   d. Undefined

22. In mathematics, factorization (British English: factorisation) or factoring is the decomposition of an object (for example, a number, a polynomial, or a matrix) into a product of other objects, or _____, which when multiplied together give the original.
   a. Thing
   b. Factors0
   c. Undefined
   d. Undefined

23. In mathematics, a _____ may be described informally as a number that can be given by an infinite decimal representation.
   a. Real number0
   b. Thing
   c. Undefined
   d. Undefined

24. A _____ is an equation in which each term is either a constant or the product of a constant times the first power of a variable.
   a. Thing
   b. Linear equation0
   c. Undefined
   d. Undefined

25. A _____ is a negotiable instrument instructing a financial institution to pay a specific amount of a specific currency from a specific demand account held in the maker/depositor's name with that institution. Both the maker and payee may be natural persons or legal entities.
   a. Check0
   b. Thing
   c. Undefined
   d. Undefined

26. A _____ is a polynomial consisting of three terms; in other words, it is the sum of three monomials.
   a. Thing
   b. Trinomial0
   c. Undefined
   d. Undefined

27. The term _____ can refer to an integer which is the square of some other integer, or an algebraic expression that can be factored as the square of some other expression.
   a. Thing
   b. Perfect square0
   c. Undefined
   d. Undefined

28. In elementary algebra, a _____ is a polynomial with two terms: the sum of two monomials. It is the simplest kind of polynomial except for a monomial.

a. Binomial0 b. Thing
c. Undefined d. Undefined

29. In mathematics and the mathematical sciences, a _____ is a fixed, but possibly unspecified, value. This is in contrast to a variable, which is not fixed.
   a. Thing b. Constant0
   c. Undefined d. Undefined

30. _____ is a fixed, but possibly unspecified, value. This is in contrast to a variable, which is not fixed.
   a. Constant term0 b. Thing
   c. Undefined d. Undefined

31. In mathematics, a _____ is a number in the form of a + bi where a and b are real numbers, and i is the imaginary unit, with the property i 2 = −1. The real number a is called the real part of the _____, and the real number b is the imaginary part.
   a. Thing b. Complex number0
   c. Undefined d. Undefined

32. In mathematics, a _____ is the result of multiplying, or an expression that identifies factors to be multiplied.
   a. Thing b. Product0
   c. Undefined d. Undefined

33. In mathematics, _____ expressions is used to reduce the expression into the lowest possible term.
   a. Thing b. Simplifying0
   c. Undefined d. Undefined

34. In algebra, a _____ is a binomial formed by taking the opposite of the second term of a binomial.
   a. Conjugate0 b. Thing
   c. Undefined d. Undefined

35. In mathematics, _____ is an elementary arithmetic operation. When one of the numbers is a whole number, _____ is the repeated sum of the other number.
   a. Multiplication0 b. Thing
   c. Undefined d. Undefined

36. A _____ is the part of a fraction that tells how many equal parts make up a whole, and which is used in the name of the fraction: "halves", "thirds", "fourths" or "quarters", "fifths" and so on.
   a. Denominator0 b. Concept
   c. Undefined d. Undefined

37. A _____ is a number that is less than zero.
   a. Negative number0 b. Thing
   c. Undefined d. Undefined

38. A _____ is a numeral used to indicate a count. The most common use of the word today is to name the part of a fraction that tells the number or count of equal parts.

a. Numerator
b. Thing
c. Undefined
d. Undefined

39. _____ is the largest positive integer that divides both numbers without remainder.
   a. Common Factor
   b. Thing
   c. Undefined
   d. Undefined

40. An _____ is a combination of numbers, operators, grouping symbols and/or free variables and bound variables arranged in a meaningful way which can be evaluated..
   a. Expression
   b. Thing
   c. Undefined
   d. Undefined

41. In mathematics, an inequality is a statement about the relative size or order of two objects. For example 14 > 10, or 14 is _____ 10.
   a. Thing
   b. Greater than
   c. Undefined
   d. Undefined

42. A _____ is a symbolic representation denoting a quantity or expression. It often represents an "unknown" quantity that has the potential to change.
   a. Variable
   b. Thing
   c. Undefined
   d. Undefined

43. A _____ is a simplified and structured visual representation of concepts, ideas, constructions, relations, statistical data, anatomy etc used in all aspects of human activities to visualize and clarify the topic.
   a. Diagram
   b. Thing
   c. Undefined
   d. Undefined

44. _____ is a relation in Euclidean geometry among the three sides of a right triangle.
   a. Thing
   b. Pythagorean Theorem
   c. Undefined
   d. Undefined

45. In mathematics, a _____ is a statement that can be proved on the basis of explicitly stated or previously agreed assumptions.
   a. Thing
   b. Theorem
   c. Undefined
   d. Undefined

46. A _____ is one of the basic shapes of geometry: a polygon with three vertices and three sides which are straight line segments.
   a. Thing
   b. Triangle
   c. Undefined
   d. Undefined

47. A _____ is the result of the addition of a set of numbers. The numbers may be natural numbers, complex numbers, matrices, or still more complicated objects. An infinite _____ is a subtle procedure known as a series.
   a. Thing
   b. Sum
   c. Undefined
   d. Undefined

Chapter 7. Quadratic Equations

48. In a right triangle, the _____ of the triangle are the two sides that are perpendicular to each other, as opposed to the hypotenuse.
    a. Thing
    b. Legs0
    c. Undefined
    d. Undefined

49. The _____ of a right triangle is the triangle's longest side; the side opposite the right angle.
    a. Thing
    b. Hypotenuse0
    c. Undefined
    d. Undefined

50. _____ has one 90° internal angle a right angle.
    a. Right triangle0
    b. Thing
    c. Undefined
    d. Undefined

51. The metre (or _____, see spelling differences) is a measure of length. It is the basic unit of length in the metric system and in the International System of Units (SI), used around the world for general and scientific purposes.
    a. Meter0
    b. Concept
    c. Undefined
    d. Undefined

52. _____ of an object is its speed in a particular direction.
    a. Velocity0
    b. Thing
    c. Undefined
    d. Undefined

53. The _____ of a solid object is the three-dimensional concept of how much space it occupies, often quantified numerically.
    a. Volume0
    b. Thing
    c. Undefined
    d. Undefined

54. In mathematics, a _____ is a two-dimensional manifold or surface that is perfectly flat.
    a. Thing
    b. Plane0
    c. Undefined
    d. Undefined

55. In mathematics, _____ are two-dimensional manifolds or surfaces that are perfectly flat.
    a. Thing
    b. Planes0
    c. Undefined
    d. Undefined

56. Initial objects are also called _____, and terminal objects are also called final.
    a. Thing
    b. Coterminal0
    c. Undefined
    d. Undefined

57. The _____ are the only integral domain whose positive elements are well-ordered, and in which order is preserved by addition. Like the natural numbers, the _____ form a countably infinite set. The set of all _____ is usually denoted in mathematics by a boldface Z .
    a. Integers0
    b. Thing
    c. Undefined
    d. Undefined

Chapter 7. Quadratic Equations

58. In mathematics, an _____, mean, or central tendency of a data set refers to a measure of the "middle" or "expected" value of the data set.
   a. Average0
   b. Concept
   c. Undefined
   d. Undefined

59. In geometry, a _____ is defined as a quadrilateral where all four of its angles are right angles.
   a. Thing
   b. Rectangle0
   c. Undefined
   d. Undefined

60. _____ is the distance around a given two-dimensional object. As a general rule, the _____ of a polygon can always be calculated by adding all the length of the sides together. So, the formula for triangles is P = a + b + c, where a, b and c stand for each side of it. For quadrilaterals the equation is P = a + b + c + d. For equilateral polygons, P = na, where n is the number of sides and a is the side length.
   a. Perimeter0
   b. Thing
   c. Undefined
   d. Undefined

61. _____ are a measure of time.
   a. Minutes0
   b. Thing
   c. Undefined
   d. Undefined

62. _____ is the transport of people on a trip/journey or the process or time involved in a person or object moving from one location to another.
   a. Thing
   b. Travel0
   c. Undefined
   d. Undefined

63. A _____ is a unit of length, usually used to measure distance, in a number of different systems, including Imperial units, United States customary units and Norwegian/Swedish mil. Its size can vary from system to system, but in each is between 1 and 10 kilometers. In contemporary English contexts _____ refers to either:
   a. Mile0
   b. Thing
   c. Undefined
   d. Undefined

64. A _____ is a special kind of ratio, indicating a relationship between two measurements with different units, such as miles to gallons or cents to pounds.
   a. Rate0
   b. Thing
   c. Undefined
   d. Undefined

65. In Euclidean geometry, a _____ is the set of all points in a plane at a fixed distance, called the radius, from a given point, the center.
   a. Thing
   b. Circle0
   c. Undefined
   d. Undefined

66. In geometry, a _____ (Greek words diairo = divide and metro = measure) of a circle is any straight line segment that passes through the centre and whose endpoints are on the circular boundary, or, in more modern usage, the length of such a line segment. When using the word in the more modern sense, one speaks of the _____ rather than a _____, because all diameters of a circle have the same length. This length is twice the radius. The _____ of a circle is also the longest chord that the circle has.

Chapter 7. Quadratic Equations

    a. Thing
    b. Diameter0
    c. Undefined
    d. Undefined

67. An _____ triange is a triangle with at least two sides of equal length.
    a. Thing
    b. Isosceles0
    c. Undefined
    d. Undefined

68. _____ has many meanings, most of which simply .
    a. Power0
    b. Thing
    c. Undefined
    d. Undefined

69. _____ variables are variables other than the independent variable that may bear any effect on the behavior of the subject being studied.
    a. Extraneous0
    b. Thing
    c. Undefined
    d. Undefined

70. In mathematics, _____ are used to indicate the square root of a number.
    a. Thing
    b. Radicals0
    c. Undefined
    d. Undefined

71. The word _____ is used in a variety of ways in mathematics.
    a. Index0
    b. Thing
    c. Undefined
    d. Undefined

72. In mathematics, the additive inverse, or _____ of a number n is the number that, when added to n, yields zero. The additive inverse of n is denoted −n. For example, 7 is −7, because 7 + (−7) = 0, and the additive inverse of −0.3 is 0.3, because −0.3 + 0.3 = 0.
    a. Opposite0
    b. Thing
    c. Undefined
    d. Undefined

73. In mathematics, the _____ of a number n is the number that, when added to n, yields zero. The _____ of n is denoted −n. For example, 7 is −7, because 7 + (−7) = 0, and the _____ of −0.3 is 0.3, because −0.3 + 0.3 = 0.
    a. Thing
    b. Additive inverse0
    c. Undefined
    d. Undefined

74. In mathematics, a _____ number is a number which can be expressed as a ratio of two integers. Non-integer _____ numbers (commonly called fractions) are usually written as the vulgar fraction a / b, where b is not zero.
    a. Thing
    b. Rational0
    c. Undefined
    d. Undefined

75. In mathematics, a _____ is a homogeneous polynomial of degree two in a number of variables.
    a. Thing
    b. Quadratic form0
    c. Undefined
    d. Undefined

76. In mathematics, there are several meanings of _____ depending on the subject.

Chapter 7. Quadratic Equations

   a. Thing
   c. Undefined
   b. Degree0
   d. Undefined

77. A _____ is a three-dimensional solid object bounded by six square faces, facets, or sides, with three meeting at each vertex.
   a. Thing
   c. Undefined
   b. Cube0
   d. Undefined

78. _____, or Rationalisation in mathematics is the process of removing a square root or imaginary number from the denominator of a fraction.
   a. Thing
   c. Undefined
   b. Rationalizing0
   d. Undefined

79. The _____ of a member of a multiset is how many memberships in the multiset it has.
   a. Thing
   c. Undefined
   b. Multiplicity0
   d. Undefined

80. A _____ is any object propelled through space by the applicationp of a force.
   a. Projectile0
   c. Undefined
   b. Thing
   d. Undefined

81. _____ are any object propelled through space by the application of a force.
   a. Thing
   c. Undefined
   b. Projectiles0
   d. Undefined

82. In mathematics, _____ allows the rapid division of any polynomial by a binomial of the form x − r. It was described by Paolo Ruffini in 1809. _____ is a special case of long division when the divisor is a linear factor.
   a. Thing
   c. Undefined
   b. Ruffini's rule0
   d. Undefined

83. The mathematical concept of a _____ expresses the intuitive idea of deterministic dependence between two quantities, one of which is viewed as primary and the other as secondary. A _____ then is a way to associate a unique output for each input of a specified type, for example, a real number or an element of a given set.
   a. Function0
   c. Undefined
   b. Thing
   d. Undefined

84. _____ is a notation for writing numbers that is often used by scientists and mathematicians to make it easier to write large and small numbers.
   a. Scientific notation0
   c. Undefined
   b. Thing
   d. Undefined

85. In linear algebra, the _____ of an n-by-n square matrix A is defined to be the sum of the elements on the main diagonal of A,
   a. Thing
   c. Undefined
   b. Trace0
   d. Undefined

Chapter 7. Quadratic Equations

86. In geographic information systems, a _____ comprises an entity with a geographic location, typically determined by points, arcs, or polygons. Carriageways and cadastres exemplify _____ data.
   a. Thing
   b. Feature0
   c. Undefined
   d. Undefined

87. In mathematics, the _____ of a function is the set of all "output" values produced by that function. Given a function $f : A \to B$, the _____ of f, is defined to be the set $\{x \in B : x = f(a) \text{ for some } a \in A\}$.
   a. Thing
   b. Range0
   c. Undefined
   d. Undefined

88. In mathematics, a _____ of a k-place relation $L \subseteq X_1 \times \ldots \times X_k$ is one of the sets X_j, $1 \leq j \leq k$. In the special case where k = 2 and $L \subseteq X_1 \times X_2$ is a function $L : X_1 \to X_2$, it is conventional to refer to X_1 as the _____ of the function and to refer to X_2 as the codomain of the function.
   a. Domain0
   b. Thing
   c. Undefined
   d. Undefined

89. In geometry, an _____ of a triangle is a straight line through a vertex and perpendicular to (i.e. forming a right angle with) the opposite side or an extension of the opposite side.
   a. Altitude0
   b. Concept
   c. Undefined
   d. Undefined

90. _____ means in succession or back-to-back
   a. Consecutive0
   b. Thing
   c. Undefined
   d. Undefined

91. Leonhard _____ was a pioneering Swiss mathematician and physicist, who spent most of his life in Russia and Germany.
   a. Person
   b. Euler0
   c. Undefined
   d. Undefined

92. In business, particularly accounting, a _____ is the time intervals that the accounts, statement, payments, or other calculations cover.
   a. Period0
   b. Thing
   c. Undefined
   d. Undefined

93. A _____ is a function that assigns a number to subsets of a given set.
   a. Measure0
   b. Thing
   c. Undefined
   d. Undefined

94. _____, Greek for "knowledge of nature," is the branch of science concerned with the discovery and characterization of universal laws which govern matter, energy, space, and time.
   a. Thing
   b. Physics0
   c. Undefined
   d. Undefined

95. The Roman Theatre._____ is a town in the Tuscany region, Italy.

84 Chapter 7. Quadratic Equations

    a. Place   b. Volterra0
    c. Undefined   d. Undefined

96. _____ is a kind of property which exists as magnitude or multitude. It is among the basic classes of things along with quality, substance, change, and relation.
    a. Amount0   b. Thing
    c. Undefined   d. Undefined

97. In mathematics, a _____ section is a curve that can be formed by intersecting a cone with a plane.
    a. Thing   b. Conic0
    c. Undefined   d. Undefined

98. Mathematical _____ is used to represent ideas.
    a. Notation0   b. Thing
    c. Undefined   d. Undefined

99. A _____ is an abstract model that uses mathematical language to describe the behavior of a system. Eykhoff defined a _____ as 'a representation of the essential aspects of an existing system which presents knowledge of that system in usable form'.
    a. Mathematical model0   b. Thing
    c. Undefined   d. Undefined

100. _____, from Latin meaning "to make progress", is defined in two different ways. Pure economic _____ is the increase in wealth that an investor has from making an investment, taking into consideration all costs associated with that investment including the opportunity cost of capital.
    a. Profit0   b. Thing
    c. Undefined   d. Undefined

101. _____ are the basic objects of study in graph theory. Informally speaking, a graph is a set of objects called points, nodes, or vertices connected by links called lines or edges.
    a. Graphs0   b. Thing
    c. Undefined   d. Undefined

102. A _____ is a polynomial function of the form $f(x) = ax^2 + bx + c$, where a, b, c are real numbers and a , 0.
    a. Event   b. Quadratic function0
    c. Undefined   d. Undefined

103. A _____ is a first degree polynomial mathematical function of the form: $f(x) = mx + b$ where m and b are real constants and x is a real variable.
    a. Linear function0   b. Thing
    c. Undefined   d. Undefined

104. _____ is a test to determine if a relation or its graph is a function or not
    a. Thing   b. Vertical line test0
    c. Undefined   d. Undefined

Chapter 7. Quadratic Equations

105. Acid _____ ratio measures the ability of a company to use its near cash or quick assets to immediately extinguish its current liabilities.
   a. Test0
   b. Thing
   c. Undefined
   d. Undefined

106. In mathematics, the concept of a _____ tries to capture the intuitive idea of a geometrical one-dimensional and continuous object. A simple example is the circle.
   a. Thing
   b. Curve0
   c. Undefined
   d. Undefined

107. In mathematics, the _____ is a conic section generated by the intersection of a right circular conical surface and a plane parallel to a generating straight line of that surface. It can also be defined as locus of points in a plane which are equidistant from a given point.
   a. Thing
   b. Parabola0
   c. Undefined
   d. Undefined

108. In geometry, a _____ is a special kind of point, usually a corner of a polygon, polyhedron, or higher dimensional polytope. In the geometry of curves a _____ is a point of where the first derivative of curvature is zero. In graph theory, a _____ is the fundamental unit out of which graphs are formed
   a. Vertex0
   b. Thing
   c. Undefined
   d. Undefined

109. _____ means "constancy", i.e. if something retains a certain feature even after we change a way of looking at it, then it is symmetric.
   a. Symmetry0
   b. Thing
   c. Undefined
   d. Undefined

110. An _____ is a straight line around which a geometric figure can be rotated.
   a. Axis0
   b. Thing
   c. Undefined
   d. Undefined

111. _____ of a two-dimensional figure is a line such that, if a perpendicular is constructed, any two points lying on the perpendicular at equal distances from the _____ are identical.
   a. Thing
   b. Axis of symmetry0
   c. Undefined
   d. Undefined

112. When _____ symmetry one can determine whether or not an object is symmetric with respect to a given mathematical operation, if, when applied to the object, this operation does not change the object or its appearance.
   a. Thing
   b. Investigating0
   c. Undefined
   d. Undefined

113. In astronomy, geography, geometry and related sciences and contexts, a plane is said to be _____ at a given point if it is locally perpendicular to the gradient of the gravity field, i.e., with the direction of the gravitational force at that point.
   a. Thing
   b. Horizontal0
   c. Undefined
   d. Undefined

Chapter 8. Quadratic Functions and Conic Sections

1. A _____ is a polynomial function of the form $f(x) = ax^2 + bx + c$, where a, b, c are real numbers and a , 0.
   a. Event
   b. Quadratic function0
   c. Undefined
   d. Undefined

2. In mathematics, the _____ is a conic section generated by the intersection of a right circular conical surface and a plane parallel to a generating straight line of that surface. It can also be defined as locus of points in a plane which are equidistant from a given point.
   a. Thing
   b. Parabola0
   c. Undefined
   d. Undefined

3. The mathematical concept of a _____ expresses the intuitive idea of deterministic dependence between two quantities, one of which is viewed as primary and the other as secondary. A _____ then is a way to associate a unique output for each input of a specified type, for example, a real number or an element of a given set.
   a. Thing
   b. Function0
   c. Undefined
   d. Undefined

4. _____ means "constancy", i.e. if something retains a certain feature even after we change a way of looking at it, then it is symmetric.
   a. Symmetry0
   b. Thing
   c. Undefined
   d. Undefined

5. An _____ is a combination of numbers, operators, grouping symbols and/or free variables and bound variables arranged in a meaningful way which can be evaluated..
   a. Expression0
   b. Thing
   c. Undefined
   d. Undefined

6. The plus and _____ signs are mathematical symbols used to represent the notions of positive and negative as well as the operations of addition and subtraction.
   a. Minus0
   b. Thing
   c. Undefined
   d. Undefined

7. In geometry, a _____ is a special kind of point, usually a corner of a polygon, polyhedron, or higher dimensional polytope. In the geometry of curves a _____ is a point of where the first derivative of curvature is zero. In graph theory, a _____ is the fundamental unit out of which graphs are formed
   a. Thing
   b. Vertex0
   c. Undefined
   d. Undefined

8. In mathematics, the _____ of a function is the set of all "output" values produced by that function. Given a function $f: A \to B$, the _____ of f, is defined to be the set $\{x \in B : x = f(a) \text{ for some } a \in A\}$.
   a. Range0
   b. Thing
   c. Undefined
   d. Undefined

9. In mathematics, a _____ of a k-place relation $L \subseteq X_1 \times \ldots \times X_k$ is one of the sets X_j, $1 \le j \le k$. In the special case where k = 2 and $L \subseteq X_1 \times X_2$ is a function $L : X_1 \to X_2$, it is conventional to refer to X_1 as the _____ of the function and to refer to X_2 as the codomain of the function.

Chapter 8. Quadratic Functions and Conic Sections

a. Thing
c. Undefined
b. Domain0
d. Undefined

10. The _____ of measurement are a globally standardized and modernized form of the metric system.
a. Thing
c. Undefined
b. Units0
d. Undefined

11. _____ are the basic objects of study in graph theory. Informally speaking, a graph is a set of objects called points, nodes, or vertices connected by links called lines or edges.
a. Thing
c. Undefined
b. Graphs0
d. Undefined

12. In astronomy, geography, geometry and related sciences and contexts, a plane is said to be _____ at a given point if it is locally perpendicular to the gradient of the gravity field, i.e., with the direction of the gravitational force at that point.
a. Thing
c. Undefined
b. Horizontal0
d. Undefined

13. One of the three formats applicable to a quadratic function is the _____ which is defined as $f = ax^2 + bx + c$.
a. Thing
c. Undefined
b. General form0
d. Undefined

14. In plane geometry, a _____ is a polygon with four equal sides, four right angles, and parallel opposite sides. In algebra, the _____ of a number is that number multiplied by itself.
a. Thing
c. Undefined
b. Square0
d. Undefined

15. _____, either of the curved-bracket punctuation marks that together make a set of _____
a. Parentheses0
c. Undefined
b. Thing
d. Undefined

16. In elementary algebra, a _____ is a polynomial with two terms: the sum of two monomials. It is the simplest kind of polynomial except for a monomial.
a. Thing
c. Undefined
b. Binomial0
d. Undefined

17. A _____ is a set of numbers that designate location in a given reference system, such as x,y in a planar _____ system or an x,y,z in a three-dimensional _____ system.
a. Coordinate0
c. Undefined
b. Thing
d. Undefined

18. In mathematics, a _____ section is a curve that can be formed by intersecting a cone with a plane.
a. Conic0
c. Undefined
b. Thing
d. Undefined

Chapter 8. Quadratic Functions and Conic Sections

19. _____ of a polynomial with real or complex coefficients is a certain expression in the coefficients of the polynomial which is equal to zero if and only if the polynomial has a multiple root i.e. a root with multiplicity greater than one in the complex numbers.
   a. Thing
   b. Discriminant0
   c. Undefined
   d. Undefined

20. In mathematics, a _____ is a homogeneous polynomial of degree two in a number of variables.
   a. Quadratic form0
   b. Thing
   c. Undefined
   d. Undefined

21. _____ is a business term for the amount of money that a company receives from its activities in a given period, mostly from sales of products and/or services to customers
   a. Revenue0
   b. Thing
   c. Undefined
   d. Undefined

22. In geometry, a _____ is defined as a quadrilateral where all four of its angles are right angles.
   a. Thing
   b. Rectangle0
   c. Undefined
   d. Undefined

23. _____ of an object is its speed in a particular direction.
   a. Velocity0
   b. Thing
   c. Undefined
   d. Undefined

24. Initial objects are also called _____, and terminal objects are also called final.
   a. Coterminal0
   b. Thing
   c. Undefined
   d. Undefined

25. A _____ is a special kind of ratio, indicating a relationship between two measurements with different units, such as miles to gallons or cents to pounds.
   a. Thing
   b. Rate0
   c. Undefined
   d. Undefined

26. In linear algebra, the _____ of an n-by-n square matrix A is defined to be the sum of the elements on the main diagonal of A,
   a. Thing
   b. Trace0
   c. Undefined
   d. Undefined

27. In geographic information systems, a _____ comprises an entity with a geographic location, typically determined by points, arcs, or polygons. Carriageways and cadastres exemplify _____ data.
   a. Thing
   b. Feature0
   c. Undefined
   d. Undefined

28. In mathematics, a _____ is a polynomial equation of the second degree. The general form is $ax^2 + bx + c = 0$.
   a. Thing
   b. Quadratic equation0
   c. Undefined
   d. Undefined

Chapter 8. Quadratic Functions and Conic Sections

29. A _____ is a one-dimensional picture in which the integers are shown as specially-marked points evenly spaced on a line.
   a. Number line0
   b. Thing
   c. Undefined
   d. Undefined

30. In mathematics, a _____ may be described informally as a number that can be given by an infinite decimal representation.
   a. Thing
   b. Real number0
   c. Undefined
   d. Undefined

31. In mathematics, an _____ is a statement about the relative size or order of two objects.
   a. Thing
   b. Inequality0
   c. Undefined
   d. Undefined

32. In mathematics, a _____ number is a number which can be expressed as a ratio of two integers. Non-integer _____ numbers (commonly called fractions) are usually written as the vulgar fraction a / b, where b is not zero.
   a. Rational0
   b. Thing
   c. Undefined
   d. Undefined

33. The word _____ comes from the Latin word linearis, which means created by lines.
   a. Thing
   b. Linear0
   c. Undefined
   d. Undefined

34. In mathematics, _____ is the decomposition of an object into a product of other objects, or factors, which when multiplied together give the original.
   a. Factoring0
   b. Thing
   c. Undefined
   d. Undefined

35. In mathematics, a _____ is an expression that is constructed from one or more variables and constants, using only the operations of addition, subtraction, multiplication, and constant positive whole number exponents. is a _____. Note in particular that division by an expression containing a variable is not in general allowed in polynomials. [1]
   a. Polynomial0
   b. Thing
   c. Undefined
   d. Undefined

36. In elementary algebra, an _____ is a set that contains every real number between two indicated numbers and may contain the two numbers themselves.
   a. Thing
   b. Interval0
   c. Undefined
   d. Undefined

37. Acid _____ ratio measures the ability of a company to use its near cash or quick assets to immediately extinguish its current liabilities.
   a. Thing
   b. Test0
   c. Undefined
   d. Undefined

38. In geometry, an _____ is a point at which a line segment or ray terminates.

Chapter 8. Quadratic Functions and Conic Sections

a. Endpoint0
b. Thing
c. Undefined
d. Undefined

39. The _____, the average in everyday English, which is also called the arithmetic _____ (and is distinguished from the geometric _____ or harmonic _____). The average is also called the sample _____. The expected value of a random variable, which is also called the population _____.

a. Thing
b. Mean0
c. Undefined
d. Undefined

40. Mathematical _____ is used to represent ideas.

a. Thing
b. Notation0
c. Undefined
d. Undefined

41. _____ is the notation in which permitted values for a variable are expressed as ranging over a certain interval; "5 < x < 9" is an example of the application of _____.

a. Interval notation0
b. Thing
c. Undefined
d. Undefined

42. In mathematics, a _____ is a constant multiplicative factor of a certain object. The object can be such things as a variable, a vector, a function, etc. For example, the _____ of $9x^2$ is 9.

a. Coefficient0
b. Thing
c. Undefined
d. Undefined

43. A quadratic equation with real solutions, called roots, which may be real or complex, is given by the _____: $x = \frac{-b \pm \sqrt{b^2 - 4ac}}{2a}$.

a. Thing
b. Quadratic formula0
c. Undefined
d. Undefined

44. In mathematics, a _____ of a complex-valued function f is a member x of the domain of f such that f(x) vanishes at x, that is, x : f (x) = 0.

a. Root0
b. Thing
c. Undefined
d. Undefined

45. A _____ is a set of possible values that a variable can take on in order to satisfy a given set of conditions, which may include equations and inequalities.

a. Solution set0
b. Thing
c. Undefined
d. Undefined

46. In mathematics, the concept of a _____ tries to capture the intuitive idea of a geometrical one-dimensional and continuous object. A simple example is the circle.

a. Thing
b. Curve0
c. Undefined
d. Undefined

47. In mathematics, a _____ is any function which can be written as the ratio of two polynomial functions.

a. Thing
b. Rational function0
c. Undefined
d. Undefined

48. _____ is the symbold used to indicate the nth root of a number
a. Thing
b. Radical0
c. Undefined
d. Undefined

49. In mathematics, _____ are used to indicate the square root of a number.
a. Radicals0
b. Thing
c. Undefined
d. Undefined

50. An _____ is a collection of two not necessarily distinct objects, one of which is distinguished as the first coordinate and the other as the second coordinate.
a. Thing
b. Ordered pair0
c. Undefined
d. Undefined

51. In mathematics, the conjugate _____ or adjoint matrix of an m-by-n matrix A with complex entries is the n-by-m matrix A* obtained from A by taking the transpose and then taking the complex conjugate of each entry.
a. Thing
b. Pairs0
c. Undefined
d. Undefined

52. In mathematics, _____ expressions is used to reduce the expression into the lowest possible term.
a. Thing
b. Simplifying0
c. Undefined
d. Undefined

53. _____ is a mathematical subject that includes the study of limits, derivatives, integrals, and power series and constitutes a major part of modern university curriculum.
a. Calculus0
b. Thing
c. Undefined
d. Undefined

54. The _____ is a measurement of how a function changes when the values of its inputs change.
a. Thing
b. Derivative0
c. Undefined
d. Undefined

55. _____ is a branch of mathematics concerning the study of structure, relation and quantity.
a. Concept
b. Algebra0
c. Undefined
d. Undefined

56. In Euclidean geometry, a _____ is moving every point a constant distance in a specified direction.
a. Concept
b. Translation0
c. Undefined
d. Undefined

57. In mathematics, the _____ of a coordinate system is the point where the axes of the system intersect.
a. Thing
b. Origin0
c. Undefined
d. Undefined

Chapter 8. Quadratic Functions and Conic Sections

58. In mathematics, a _____ (also spelled reflexion) is a map that transforms an object into its mirror image.
   a. Reflection0
   b. Concept
   c. Undefined
   d. Undefined

59. In mathematics, _____ are the intuitive idea of a geometrical one-dimensional and continuous object.
   a. Thing
   b. Curves0
   c. Undefined
   d. Undefined

60. In mathematics, a _____ is a two-dimensional manifold or surface that is perfectly flat.
   a. Thing
   b. Plane0
   c. Undefined
   d. Undefined

61. A _____ is a three-dimensional geometric shape formed by straight lines through a fixed point (vertex) to the points of a fixed curve (directrix)
   a. Concept
   b. Cone0
   c. Undefined
   d. Undefined

62. In mathematics and its applications, a _____ is a system for assigning an n-tuple of numbers or scalars to each point in an n-dimensional space.
   a. Coordinate system0
   b. Concept
   c. Undefined
   d. Undefined

63. _____ means of or relating to the French philosopher and mathematician René Descartes.
   a. Cartesian0
   b. Thing
   c. Undefined
   d. Undefined

64. In mathematics, the _____ is used to determine each point uniquely in a plane through two numbers, usually called the x-coordinate and the y-coordinate of the point.
   a. Thing
   b. Cartesian coordinate system0
   c. Undefined
   d. Undefined

65. _____ is often used to describe the measurement of the steepness, incline, gradient, or grade of a straight line. The _____ is defined as the ratio of the "rise" divided by the "run" between two points on a line, or in other words, the ratio of the altitude change to the horizontal distance between any two points on the line.
   a. Thing
   b. Slope0
   c. Undefined
   d. Undefined

66. A _____ is an equation in which each term is either a constant or the product of a constant times the first power of a variable.
   a. Thing
   b. Linear equation0
   c. Undefined
   d. Undefined

67. _____ is a test to determine if a relation or its graph is a function or not
   a. Thing
   b. Vertical line test0
   c. Undefined
   d. Undefined

68. In mathematics, a _____ of a number x is a number r such that r^2 = x, or in words, a number r whose square (the result of multiplying the number by itself) is x.
   a. Thing
   b. Square root0
   c. Undefined
   d. Undefined

69. In geometry, the _____ of an object is a point in some sense in the middle of the object.
   a. Thing
   b. Center0
   c. Undefined
   d. Undefined

70. In Euclidean geometry, a _____ is the set of all points in a plane at a fixed distance, called the radius, from a given point, the center.
   a. Thing
   b. Circle0
   c. Undefined
   d. Undefined

71. In classical geometry, a _____ of a circle or sphere is any line segment from its center to its boundary. By extension, the _____ of a circle or sphere is the length of any such segment. The _____ is half the diameter. In science and engineering the term _____ of curvature is commonly used as a synonym for _____.
   a. Radius0
   b. Thing
   c. Undefined
   d. Undefined

72. A _____ is one of the basic shapes of geometry: a polygon with three vertices and three sides which are straight line segments.
   a. Thing
   b. Triangle0
   c. Undefined
   d. Undefined

73. A _____ is the result of the addition of a set of numbers. The numbers may be natural numbers, complex numbers, matrices, or still more complicated objects. An infinite _____ is a subtle procedure known as a series.
   a. Thing
   b. Sum0
   c. Undefined
   d. Undefined

74. In a right triangle, the _____ of the triangle are the two sides that are perpendicular to each other, as opposed to the hypotenuse.
   a. Legs0
   b. Thing
   c. Undefined
   d. Undefined

75. The _____ of a right triangle is the triangle's longest side; the side opposite the right angle.
   a. Thing
   b. Hypotenuse0
   c. Undefined
   d. Undefined

76. _____ has one 90° internal angle a right angle.
   a. Thing
   b. Right triangle0
   c. Undefined
   d. Undefined

77. In mathematics, the _____ (or modulus) of a real number is its numerical value without regard to its sign.

a. Absolute value0 b. Thing
c. Undefined d. Undefined

78. A _____ is a deliberate process for transforming one or more inputs into one or more results.
a. Thing b. Calculation0
c. Undefined d. Undefined

79. _____ is a relation in Euclidean geometry among the three sides of a right triangle.
a. Thing b. Pythagorean Theorem0
c. Undefined d. Undefined

80. In geometry, a line _____ is a part of a line that is bounded by two end points, and contains every point on the line between its end points.
a. Concept b. Segment0
c. Undefined d. Undefined

81. A _____ is a part of a line that is bounded by two end points, and contains every point on the line between its end points.
a. Line segment0 b. Thing
c. Undefined d. Undefined

82. In mathematics, a _____ is a statement that can be proved on the basis of explicitly stated or previously agreed assumptions.
a. Thing b. Theorem0
c. Undefined d. Undefined

83. _____ is the middle point of a line segment.
a. Midpoint0 b. Thing
c. Undefined d. Undefined

84. In geometry, a _____ (Greek words diairo = divide and metro = measure) of a circle is any straight line segment that passes through the centre and whose endpoints are on the circular boundary, or, in more modern usage, the length of such a line segment. When using the word in the more modern sense, one speaks of the _____ rather than a _____, because all diameters of a circle have the same length. This length is twice the radius. The _____ of a circle is also the longest chord that the circle has.
a. Diameter0 b. Thing
c. Undefined d. Undefined

85. _____ is a notation for writing numbers that is often used by scientists and mathematicians to make it easier to write large and small numbers.
a. Scientific notation0 b. Thing
c. Undefined d. Undefined

86. A _____ is a quantity that denotes the proportional amount or magnitude of one quantity relative to another.

Chapter 8. Quadratic Functions and Conic Sections

a. Ratio0
b. Thing
c. Undefined
d. Undefined

87. In geometry, an _____ polygon is a polygon which has all sides of the same length.
    a. Thing
    b. Equilateral0
    c. Undefined
    d. Undefined

88. An _____ is a triangle in which all sides are of equal length.
    a. Thing
    b. Equilateral triangle0
    c. Undefined
    d. Undefined

89. A _____ can refer to a line joining two nonadjacent vertices of a polygon or polyhedron, or in some contexts any upward or downward sloping line. .
    a. Thing
    b. Diagonal0
    c. Undefined
    d. Undefined

90. An _____ triange is a triangle with at least two sides of equal length.
    a. Isosceles0
    b. Thing
    c. Undefined
    d. Undefined

91. _____ is the distance around a given two-dimensional object. As a general rule, the _____ of a polygon can always be calculated by adding all the length of the sides together. So, the formula for triangles is P = a + b + c, where a, b and c stand for each side of it. For quadrilaterals the equation is P = a + b + c + d. For equilateral polygons, P = na, where n is the number of sides and a is the side length.
    a. Perimeter0
    b. Thing
    c. Undefined
    d. Undefined

92. In mathematics, an _____ .
    a. Thing
    b. Ellipse0
    c. Undefined
    d. Undefined

93. In mathematics and the mathematical sciences, a _____ is a fixed, but possibly unspecified, value. This is in contrast to a variable, which is not fixed.
    a. Thing
    b. Constant0
    c. Undefined
    d. Undefined

94. In geometry, the _____ are a pair of special points used in describing conic sections. The four types of conic sections are the circle, parabola, ellipse, and hyperbola.
    a. Thing
    b. Foci0
    c. Undefined
    d. Undefined

95. _____ is the scientific study of celestial objects such as stars, planets, comets, and galaxies; and phenomena that originate outside the Earth's atmosphere.
    a. Thing
    b. Astronomy0
    c. Undefined
    d. Undefined

Chapter 8. Quadratic Functions and Conic Sections

96. An _____ is a straight line around which a geometric figure can be rotated.
 a. Axis0 b. Thing
 c. Undefined d. Undefined

97. In linear algebra, a _____ of a matrix A is the determinant of some smaller square matrix, cut down from A.
 a. Thing b. Minor0
 c. Undefined d. Undefined

98. In mathematics, a _____ is a type of conic section defined as the intersection between a right circular conical surface and a plane which cuts through both halves of the cone.
 a. Hyperbola0 b. Thing
 c. Undefined d. Undefined

99. An _____ is a straight line or curve A to which another curve B approaches closer and closer as one moves along it. As one moves along B, the space between it and the _____ A becomes smaller and smaller, and can in fact be made as small as one could wish by going far enough along. A curve may or may not touch or cross its _____. In fact, the curve may intersect the _____ an infinite number of times.
 a. Thing b. Asymptote0
 c. Undefined d. Undefined

100. _____ the expected value of a random variable displays the average or central value of the variable. It is a summary value of the distribution of the variable.
 a. Determining0 b. Thing
 c. Undefined d. Undefined

101. In mathematics, the _____ of two sets A and B is the set that contains all elements of A that also belong to B (or equivalently, all elements of B that also belong to A), but no other elements.
 a. Intersection0 b. Thing
 c. Undefined d. Undefined

102. _____ are a set of equations containing multiple variables.
 a. Thing b. Systems of equations0
 c. Undefined d. Undefined

103. _____ systems represent systems whose behavior is not expressible as a sum of the behaviors of its descriptors.
 a. Nonlinear0 b. Thing
 c. Undefined d. Undefined

104. A _____ represents a system whose behavior is not expressible as a sum of the behaviors of its descriptors.
 a. Nonlinear system0 b. Thing
 c. Undefined d. Undefined

105. The word _____ is used in a variety of ways in mathematics.

a. Thing
b. Index0
c. Undefined
d. Undefined

106. In mathematics, a _____ is the end result of a division problem. It can also be expressed as the number of times the divisor divides into the dividend.
   a. Thing
   b. Quotient0
   c. Undefined
   d. Undefined

107. The function difference divided by the point difference is known as the _____
   a. Thing
   b. Difference quotient0
   c. Undefined
   d. Undefined

108. _____ of a two-dimensional figure is a line such that, if a perpendicular is constructed, any two points lying on the perpendicular at equal distances from the _____ are identical.
   a. Axis of symmetry0
   b. Thing
   c. Undefined
   d. Undefined

109. In mathematics, an _____, mean, or central tendency of a data set refers to a measure of the "middle" or "expected" value of the data set.
   a. Concept
   b. Average0
   c. Undefined
   d. Undefined

110. A _____ is the part of the dividend that is left over when the dividend is not evenly divisible by the divisor.
   a. Thing
   b. Remainder0
   c. Undefined
   d. Undefined

111. _____ in algebra is an application of polynomial long division.
   a. Remainder theorem0
   b. Thing
   c. Undefined
   d. Undefined

112. In mathematics, _____ allows the rapid division of any polynomial by a binomial of the form x − r. It was described by Paolo Ruffini in 1809. _____ is a special case of long division when the divisor is a linear factor.
   a. Thing
   b. Ruffini's rule0
   c. Undefined
   d. Undefined

Chapter 9. Exponential and Logarithmic Functions

1. In mathematics, a _____ of a number x is the exponent y of the power by such that $x = b^y$. The value used for the base b must be neither 0 nor 1, nor a root of 1 in the case of the extension to complex numbers, and is typically 10, e, or 2.
   a. Thing
   b. Logarithm0
   c. Undefined
   d. Undefined

2. A _____ is a deliberate process for transforming one or more inputs into one or more results.
   a. Thing
   b. Calculation0
   c. Undefined
   d. Undefined

3. The mathematical concept of a _____ expresses the intuitive idea of deterministic dependence between two quantities, one of which is viewed as primary and the other as secondary. A _____ then is a way to associate a unique output for each input of a specified type, for example, a real number or an element of a given set.
   a. Function0
   b. Thing
   c. Undefined
   d. Undefined

4. John _____ of Merchistoun , nicknamed Marvellous Merchistoun, was a Scottish mathematician, physicist, astronomer/astrologer and 8th Laird of Merchistoun. He is most remembered as the inventor of logarithms and _____'s bones, and for popularizing the use of the decimal point.
   a. Napier0
   b. Person
   c. Undefined
   d. Undefined

5. _____ of Nerchistoun, nicknamed Marvellous Merchistoun, was a Scottish mathematician, physicist, astronomer/astrologer and 8th Laird of Merchistoun.
   a. John Napier0
   b. Person
   c. Undefined
   d. Undefined

6. _____ is the logarithm to the base e, where e is an irrational constant approximately equal to 2.718281828459.
   a. Natural logarithm0
   b. Thing
   c. Undefined
   d. Undefined

7. _____ is a set of numbers, in the broadest sense of the word, together with one or more operations, such as addition or multiplication.
   a. Number system0
   b. Thing
   c. Undefined
   d. Undefined

8. In mathematics, _____ expressions is used to reduce the expression into the lowest possible term.
   a. Thing
   b. Simplifying0
   c. Undefined
   d. Undefined

9. _____ is the fee paid on borrowed money.
   a. Interest0
   b. Thing
   c. Undefined
   d. Undefined

10. _____ is a straight line or curve A to which another curve B the one being studied approaches closer and closer as one moves along it.

Chapter 9. Exponential and Logarithmic Functions

a. Thing
c. Undefined
b. Vertical asymptote0
d. Undefined

11. Mathematical _____ is used to represent ideas.
a. Notation0
c. Undefined
b. Thing
d. Undefined

12. An _____ is a straight line or curve A to which another curve B approaches closer and closer as one moves along it. As one moves along B, the space between it and the _____ A becomes smaller and smaller, and can in fact be made as small as one could wish by going far enough along. A curve may or may not touch or cross its _____. In fact, the curve may intersect the _____ an infinite number of times.
a. Thing
c. Undefined
b. Asymptote0
d. Undefined

13. In astronomy, geography, geometry and related sciences and contexts, a plane is said to be _____ at a given point if it is locally perpendicular to the gradient of the gravity field, i.e., with the direction of the gravitational force at that point.
a. Horizontal0
c. Undefined
b. Thing
d. Undefined

14. In mathematics, _____ growth occurs when the growth rate of a function is always proportional to the function's current size.
a. Thing
c. Undefined
b. Exponential0
d. Undefined

15. _____ is one of the most important functions in mathematics. A function commonly used to study growth and decay
a. Exponential function0
c. Undefined
b. Thing
d. Undefined

16. A _____ number is a positive integer which has a positive divisor other than one or itself.
a. Composite0
c. Undefined
b. Thing
d. Undefined

17. _____ element of an element x with respect to a binary operation * with identity element e is an element y such that x * y = y * x = e. In particular,
a. Inverse0
c. Undefined
b. Thing
d. Undefined

18. An _____ is a function which does the reverse of a given function.
a. Inverse function0
c. Undefined
b. Thing
d. Undefined

19. The act of _____ is the calculated approximation of a result which is usable even if input data may be incomplete, uncertain, or noisy.

Chapter 9. Exponential and Logarithmic Functions

    a. Estimating0
    b. Thing
    c. Undefined
    d. Undefined

20. An _____ is a combination of numbers, operators, grouping symbols and/or free variables and bound variables arranged in a meaningful way which can be evaluated..
    a. Expression0
    b. Thing
    c. Undefined
    d. Undefined

21. In mathematics, _____ occurs when the growth rate of a function is always proportional to the function's current size.
    a. Exponential growth0
    b. Thing
    c. Undefined
    d. Undefined

22. _____ is a term used in accounting, economics and finance with reference to the fact that assets with finite lives lose value over time.
    a. Thing
    b. Depreciation0
    c. Undefined
    d. Undefined

23. In mathematics, the concept of a _____ tries to capture the intuitive idea of a geometrical one-dimensional and continuous object. A simple example is the circle.
    a. Curve0
    b. Thing
    c. Undefined
    d. Undefined

24. In mathematics, _____ are the intuitive idea of a geometrical one-dimensional and continuous object.
    a. Curves0
    b. Thing
    c. Undefined
    d. Undefined

25. The _____ refers to a relationship between the duration of learning or experience and the resulting progress
    a. Thing
    b. Learning curve0
    c. Undefined
    d. Undefined

26. A _____ is the result of the addition of a set of numbers. The numbers may be natural numbers, complex numbers, matrices, or still more complicated objects. An infinite _____ is a subtle procedure known as a series.
    a. Sum0
    b. Thing
    c. Undefined
    d. Undefined

27. In mathematics, a _____ of a k-place relation $L \subseteq X_1 \times ... \times X_k$ is one of the sets X_j, $1 \leq j \leq k$. In the special case where k = 2 and $L \subseteq X_1 \times X_2$ is a function $L : X_1 \rightarrow X_2$, it is conventional to refer to X_1 as the _____ of the function and to refer to X_2 as the codomain of the function.
    a. Domain0
    b. Thing
    c. Undefined
    d. Undefined

28. In mathematics, a _____ is the result of multiplying, or an expression that identifies factors to be multiplied.
    a. Product0
    b. Thing
    c. Undefined
    d. Undefined

29. In mathematics, a _____ is the end result of a division problem. It can also be expressed as the number of times the divisor divides into the dividend.
   a. Quotient0
   b. Thing
   c. Undefined
   d. Undefined

30. In mathematics, a _____ may be described informally as a number that can be given by an infinite decimal representation.
   a. Thing
   b. Real number0
   c. Undefined
   d. Undefined

31. In elementary algebra, an _____ is a set that contains every real number between two indicated numbers and may contain the two numbers themselves.
   a. Interval0
   b. Thing
   c. Undefined
   d. Undefined

32. _____ are the basic objects of study in graph theory. Informally speaking, a graph is a set of objects called points, nodes, or vertices connected by links called lines or edges.
   a. Thing
   b. Graphs0
   c. Undefined
   d. Undefined

33. In mathematics, the _____ of a function is the set of all "output" values produced by that function. Given a function $f : A \to B$, the _____ of f, is defined to be the set $\{x \in B : x = f(a) \text{ for some } a \in A\}$.
   a. Range0
   b. Thing
   c. Undefined
   d. Undefined

34. In Euclidean geometry, a _____ is moving every point a constant distance in a specified direction.
   a. Translation0
   b. Concept
   c. Undefined
   d. Undefined

35. In mathematics, a _____ of a positive integer n is a way of writing n as a sum of positive integers.
   a. Thing
   b. Composition0
   c. Undefined
   d. Undefined

36. _____ is a test to determine if a relation or its graph is a function or not
   a. Vertical line test0
   b. Thing
   c. Undefined
   d. Undefined

37. Acid _____ ratio measures the ability of a company to use its near cash or quick assets to immediately extinguish its current liabilities.
   a. Thing
   b. Test0
   c. Undefined
   d. Undefined

38. _____ is a test used to determine if a function is injective, surjective or bijective.
   a. Horizontal line test0
   b. Thing
   c. Undefined
   d. Undefined

Chapter 9. Exponential and Logarithmic Functions

39. An _____ is a collection of two not necessarily distinct objects, one of which is distinguished as the first coordinate and the other as the second coordinate.
   a. Ordered pair0
   b. Thing
   c. Undefined
   d. Undefined

40. In mathematics, the conjugate _____ or adjoint matrix of an m-by-n matrix A with complex entries is the n-by-m matrix A* obtained from A by taking the transpose and then taking the complex conjugate of each entry.
   a. Thing
   b. Pairs0
   c. Undefined
   d. Undefined

41. In mathematics, a _____ (also spelled reflexion) is a map that transforms an object into its mirror image.
   a. Concept
   b. Reflection0
   c. Undefined
   d. Undefined

42. _____ means "constancy", i.e. if something retains a certain feature even after we change a way of looking at it, then it is symmetric.
   a. Symmetry0
   b. Thing
   c. Undefined
   d. Undefined

43. An _____ is when two lines intersect somewhere on a plane creating a right angle at intersection
   a. Axes0
   b. Thing
   c. Undefined
   d. Undefined

44. The population _____ is the total number of human beings alive on the planet Earth at a given time.
   a. Of the world0
   b. Thing
   c. Undefined
   d. Undefined

45. In sociology and biology a _____ is the collection of people or organisms of a particular species living in a given geographic area or space, usually measured by a census.
   a. Thing
   b. Population0
   c. Undefined
   d. Undefined

46. The _____ is the total number of human beings alive on the planet Earth at a given time.
   a. Population of the world0
   b. Thing
   c. Undefined
   d. Undefined

47. A _____ is a polynomial function of the form f(x) = ax^2 + bx +c , where a, b, c are real numbers and a , 0.
   a. Event
   b. Quadratic function0
   c. Undefined
   d. Undefined

48. A _____ is a symbolic representation denoting a quantity or expression. It often represents an "unknown" quantity that has the potential to change.
   a. Variable0
   b. Thing
   c. Undefined
   d. Undefined

49. _____ is a synonym for information.

Chapter 9. Exponential and Logarithmic Functions

a. Thing
c. Undefined
b. Data0
d. Undefined

50. In mathematics and the mathematical sciences, a _____ is a fixed, but possibly unspecified, value. This is in contrast to a variable, which is not fixed.
a. Constant0
c. Undefined
b. Thing
d. Undefined

51. In mathematics, an inequality is a statement about the relative size or order of two objects. For example 14 > 10, or 14 is _____ 10.
a. Greater than0
c. Undefined
b. Thing
d. Undefined

52. _____ is a decrease that follows an exponential function.
a. Thing
c. Undefined
b. Exponential decay0
d. Undefined

53. _____ interest refers to the fact that whenever interest is calculated, it is based not only on the original principal, but also on any unpaid interest that has been added to the principal.
a. Thing
c. Undefined
b. Compound0
d. Undefined

54. _____ refers to the fact that whenever interest is calculated, it is based not only on the original principal, but also on any unpaid interest that has been added to the principal. The more frequently interest is compounded, the faster the balance grows.
a. Concept
c. Undefined
b. Compound interest0
d. Undefined

55. _____ is a kind of property which exists as magnitude or multitude. It is among the basic classes of things along with quality, substance, change, and relation.
a. Amount0
c. Undefined
b. Thing
d. Undefined

56. A _____ is a special kind of ratio, indicating a relationship between two measurements with different units, such as miles to gallons or cents to pounds.
a. Thing
c. Undefined
b. Rate0
d. Undefined

57. A _____ is a type of debt. All material things can be lent but this article focuses exclusively on monetary loans. Like all debt instruments, a _____ entails the redistribution of financial assets over time, between the lender and the borrower.
a. Loan0
c. Undefined
b. Thing
d. Undefined

58. _____ or investing is a term with several closely-related meanings in business management, finance and economics, related to saving or deferring consumption.

Chapter 9. Exponential and Logarithmic Functions

a. Thing
b. Investment0
c. Undefined
d. Undefined

59. _____ is the state of being greater than any finite number, however large.
a. Thing
b. Infinity0
c. Undefined
d. Undefined

60. Initial objects are also called _____, and terminal objects are also called final.
a. Thing
b. Coterminal0
c. Undefined
d. Undefined

61. A _____ are accounts maintained by commercial banks, savings and loan associations, credit unions, and mutual savings banks that pay interest but can not be used directly as money by, for example, writing a cheque.
a. Thing
b. Savings account0
c. Undefined
d. Undefined

62. The _____ of measurement are a globally standardized and modernized form of the metric system.
a. Units0
b. Thing
c. Undefined
d. Undefined

63. _____ is a business term for the amount of money that a company receives from its activities in a given period, mostly from sales of products and/or services to customers
a. Revenue0
b. Thing
c. Undefined
d. Undefined

64. _____ is a mathematical science pertaining to the collection, analysis, interpretation or explanation, and presentation of data. It is applicable to a wide variety of academic disciplines, from the physical and social sciences to the humanities.
a. Statistics0
b. Thing
c. Undefined
d. Undefined

65. The Yakovlev Yak-25, NATO designation _____-A / Mandrake, was a swept wing, turbojet-powered interceptor aircraft and reconnaissance aircraft used by the Soviet Union.
a. Thing
b. Flashlight0
c. Undefined
d. Undefined

66. In mathematics, the _____ is the logarithm with base 10.
a. Common logarithm0
b. Thing
c. Undefined
d. Undefined

67. Equivalence is the condition of being _____ or essentially equal.
a. Thing
b. Equivalent0
c. Undefined
d. Undefined

68. _____, either of the curved-bracket punctuation marks that together make a set of _____

Chapter 9. Exponential and Logarithmic Functions

    a. Parentheses0
    c. Undefined
    b. Thing
    d. Undefined

69. _____ is a mathematical operation, written a^n, involving two numbers, the base a and the exponent n.
    a. Thing
    b. Exponentiating0
    c. Undefined
    d. Undefined

70. _____ is a mathematical operation, written a^n, involving two numbers, the base a and the exponent n.
    a. Thing
    b. Exponentiation0
    c. Undefined
    d. Undefined

71. _____ is the state of being greater than any finite real or natural number, however large.
    a. Infinite0
    b. Thing
    c. Undefined
    d. Undefined

72. In mathematics, an _____ number is any real number that is not a rational number- that is, it is a number which cannot be expressed as a fraction m/n, where m and n are integers.
    a. Thing
    b. Irrational0
    c. Undefined
    d. Undefined

73. In mathematics, an _____ is any real number that is not a rational number ¡ª that is, it is a number which cannot be expressed as m/n, where m and n are integers.
    a. Irrational number0
    b. Thing
    c. Undefined
    d. Undefined

74. In mathematics, _____ are any real number that is not a rational number ¡ª that is, it is a number which cannot be expressed as m/n, where m and n are integers.
    a. Thing
    b. Irrational numbers0
    c. Undefined
    d. Undefined

75. A _____ is a set of numbers that designate location in a given reference system, such as x,y in a planar _____ system or an x,y,z in a three-dimensional _____ system.
    a. Coordinate0
    b. Thing
    c. Undefined
    d. Undefined

76. A _____ is a negotiable instrument instructing a financial institution to pay a specific amount of a specific currency from a specific demand account held in the maker/depositor's name with that institution. Both the maker and payee may be natural persons or legal entities.
    a. Check0
    b. Thing
    c. Undefined
    d. Undefined

77. The _____, the average in everyday English, which is also called the arithmetic _____ (and is distinguished from the geometric _____ or harmonic _____). The average is also called the sample _____. The expected value of a random variable, which is also called the population _____.

a. Mean0
b. Thing
c. Undefined
d. Undefined

78. In mathematics, defined and _____ are used to explain whether or not expressions have meaningful, sensible, and unambiguous values.
    a. Thing
    b. Undefined0
    c. Undefined
    d. Undefined

79. A _____ is a number that is less than zero.
    a. Thing
    b. Negative number0
    c. Undefined
    d. Undefined

80. The _____ governs the differentiation of products of differentiable functions.
    a. Product rule0
    b. Thing
    c. Undefined
    d. Undefined

81. In mathematics, factorization (British English: factorisation) or factoring is the decomposition of an object (for example, a number, a polynomial, or a matrix) into a product of other objects, or _____, which when multiplied together give the original.
    a. Factors0
    b. Thing
    c. Undefined
    d. Undefined

82. In mathematics, a _____ is a demonstration that, assuming certain axioms, some statement is necessarily true.
    a. Proof0
    b. Thing
    c. Undefined
    d. Undefined

83. _____ is the process of reducing the number of significant digits in a number.
    a. Rounding0
    b. Concept
    c. Undefined
    d. Undefined

84. In mathematics, _____ is an elementary arithmetic operation. When one of the numbers is a whole number, _____ is the repeated sum of the other number.
    a. Multiplication0
    b. Thing
    c. Undefined
    d. Undefined

85. _____ has many meanings, most of which simply .
    a. Thing
    b. Power0
    c. Undefined
    d. Undefined

86. _____ is a method for differentiating expressions involving exponentiation the power operation.
    a. Power rule0
    b. Thing
    c. Undefined
    d. Undefined

87. _____ traditionally refers to the statistical process of determining comparable scores on different forms of an exam

Chapter 9. Exponential and Logarithmic Functions

    a. Equating0
    c. Undefined
    b. Thing
    d. Undefined

88. The _____ is a method of finding the derivative of a function that is the quotient of two other functions for which derivatives exist.
    a. Thing
    c. Undefined
    b. Quotient rule0
    d. Undefined

89. In mathematics, _____ is the decomposition of an object into a product of other objects, or factors, which when multiplied together give the original.
    a. Thing
    c. Undefined
    b. Factoring0
    d. Undefined

90. A _____ is a numeral used to indicate a count. The most common use of the word today is to name the part of a fraction that tells the number or count of equal parts.
    a. Numerator0
    c. Undefined
    b. Thing
    d. Undefined

91. _____ refers to the reduction of the body of a formerly living organism into simpler forms of matter.
    a. Decomposing0
    c. Undefined
    b. Thing
    d. Undefined

92. Sir Isaac _____, was an English physicist, mathematician, astronomer, natural philosopher, and alchemist, regarded by many as the greatest figure in the history of science
    a. Person
    c. Undefined
    b. Newton0
    d. Undefined

93. In Euclidean geometry, a uniform _____ is a linear transformation that enlargers or diminishes objects, and whose _____ factor is the same in all directions. This is also called homothethy.
    a. Scale0
    c. Undefined
    b. Thing
    d. Undefined

94. An _____ is the result from the sudden release of stored energy in the Earth's crust that creates seismic waves.
    a. Earthquake0
    c. Undefined
    b. Thing
    d. Undefined

95. A _____ is a quantity that denotes the proportional amount or magnitude of one quantity relative to another.
    a. Thing
    c. Undefined
    b. Ratio0
    d. Undefined

96. In grammar, the _____ is the form of an adjective or adverb which denotes the degree or grade by which a person, thing, or other entity has a property or quality greater or less in extent than that of another.
    a. Comparative0
    c. Undefined
    b. Thing
    d. Undefined

Chapter 9. Exponential and Logarithmic Functions

97. _____ is the process in which an unstable atomic nucleus loses energy by emitting radiation in the form of particles or electromagnetic waves.
   a. Radioactive decay0
   b. Thing
   c. Undefined
   d. Undefined

98. In geometry, an _____ of a triangle is a straight line through a vertex and perpendicular to (i.e. forming a right angle with) the opposite side or an extension of the opposite side.
   a. Altitude0
   b. Concept
   c. Undefined
   d. Undefined

99. _____ is a physical property of a system that underlies the common notions of hot and cold; something that is hotter has the greater _____.
   a. Thing
   b. Temperature0
   c. Undefined
   d. Undefined

100. In mathematics, a _____ is an n-tuple with n being 3.
   a. Triple0
   b. Thing
   c. Undefined
   d. Undefined

101. A _____ function is a function for which, intuitively, small changes in the input result in small changes in the output.
   a. Event
   b. Continuous0
   c. Undefined
   d. Undefined

102. An _____ is the fee paid on borrow money.
   a. Interest rate0
   b. Concept
   c. Undefined
   d. Undefined

103. The word _____ comes from the Latin word linearis, which means created by lines.
   a. Thing
   b. Linear0
   c. Undefined
   d. Undefined

104. The word _____ is used in a variety of ways in mathematics.
   a. Thing
   b. Index0
   c. Undefined
   d. Undefined

105. A _____, formed by the composition of one function on another, represents the application of the former to the result of the application of the latter to the argument of the composite.
   a. Composite function0
   b. Thing
   c. Undefined
   d. Undefined

106. The _____ functions is determined by the nesting of two or more functions to form a single new function.
   a. Composition of two0
   b. Thing
   c. Undefined
   d. Undefined

107. _____ is the estimation of a physical quantity such as distance, energy, temperature, or time.

Chapter 9. Exponential and Logarithmic Functions

a. Measurement0
b. Thing
c. Undefined
d. Undefined

108. In geometry, the _____ of an object is a point in some sense in the middle of the object.
   a. Thing
   b. Center0
   c. Undefined
   d. Undefined

109. In Euclidean geometry, a _____ is the set of all points in a plane at a fixed distance, called the radius, from a given point, the center.
   a. Circle0
   b. Thing
   c. Undefined
   d. Undefined

110. _____ are a set of equations containing multiple variables.
   a. Systems of equations0
   b. Thing
   c. Undefined
   d. Undefined

111. In mathematics, the _____ of two sets A and B is the set that contains all elements of A that also belong to B (or equivalently, all elements of B that also belong to A), but no other elements.
   a. Thing
   b. Intersection0
   c. Undefined
   d. Undefined

112. A _____ is a unit of length, usually used to measure distance, in a number of different systems, including Imperial units, United States customary units and Norwegian/Swedish mil. Its size can vary from system to system, but in each is between 1 and 10 kilometers. In contemporary English contexts _____ refers to either:
   a. Mile0
   b. Thing
   c. Undefined
   d. Undefined

113. In mathematics, an _____, mean, or central tendency of a data set refers to a measure of the "middle" or "expected" value of the data set.
   a. Concept
   b. Average0
   c. Undefined
   d. Undefined

114. _____ is the transport of people on a trip/journey or the process or time involved in a person or object moving from one location to another.
   a. Travel0
   b. Thing
   c. Undefined
   d. Undefined

115. A _____ is one of the basic shapes of geometry: a polygon with three vertices and three sides which are straight line segments.
   a. Thing
   b. Triangle0
   c. Undefined
   d. Undefined

116. _____ is the distance around a given two-dimensional object. As a general rule, the _____ of a polygon can always be calculated by adding all the length of the sides together. So, the formula for triangles is P = a + b + c, where a, b and c stand for each side of it. For quadrilaterals the equation is P = a + b + c + d. For equilateral polygons, P = na, where n is the number of sides and a is the side length.

a. Perimeter0
b. Thing
c. Undefined
d. Undefined

117. _____ has one 90° internal angle a right angle.
a. Thing
b. Right triangle0
c. Undefined
d. Undefined

118. _____ of an object is its speed in a particular direction.
a. Velocity0
b. Thing
c. Undefined
d. Undefined

119. _____ is the force that opposes the relative motion or tendency toward such motion of two surfaces in contact.
a. Thing
b. Friction0
c. Undefined
d. Undefined

Chapter 10. Sequences, Series, and the Binomial Theorem

1. A _____ is simply a polynomial with two terms such as this example: 2x + 7.
   a. Binomial10
   b. -equivalence
   c. Undefined
   d. Undefined

2. The Greek letter _____ indicates summation.
   a. -equivalence
   b. Sigma10
   c. Undefined
   d. Undefined

3. Addition (or summation) is one of the basic operations of arithmetic. In its simplest form, addition combines two numbers, the augend and addend, into a single number, the _____. Adding more numbers can be viewed as repeated addition. (Repeated addition of the number one is the most basic form of counting.) By extension, the addition of zero numbers, one number, or infinitely many numbers can be defined.
   a. Sum10
   b. -equivalence
   c. Undefined
   d. Undefined

4. A _____ is a number or variable, or the product or quotient of a number or variable.
   a. Term10
   b. -equivalence
   c. Undefined
   d. Undefined

5. _____ consist of the positive natural numbers (1, 2, 3, ...), their negatives (−1, −2, −3, ...) and the number zero.
   a. ADE classification
   b. Integers10
   c. Undefined
   d. Undefined

6. An _____ combines numbers, operators, and/or variables but contains no equal or inequality sign.
   a. ADE classification
   b. Expression10
   c. Undefined
   d. Undefined

7. The _____ in a disttribution or in an interval is the least value.
   a. Lower limit10
   b. -equivalence
   c. Undefined
   d. Undefined

8. _____ or arithmetics (from the Greek word áñéèìüò = number) in common usage is a branch of (or the forerunner of) mathematics which records elementary properties of certain operations on numerals, though in usage by professional mathematicians, it often is treated as a synonym for number theory.
   a. Arithmetic10
   b. ADE classification
   c. Undefined
   d. Undefined

9. A number that does not change in value in a given situation is a _____.
   a. Constant10
   b. -equivalence
   c. Undefined
   d. Undefined

10. A _____ is a positive integer (1,2,3,...).
    a. Natural number10
    b. -equivalence
    c. Undefined
    d. Undefined

Chapter 10. Sequences, Series, and the Binomial Theorem

11. A _____ is the relationship between two quantities. It is expressed as the quotient of two numbers, or as two numbers separated by a colon (pronounced "to"). A number that can be written as a _____ of two integers is a rational number.
   a. Ratio10
   b. -equivalence
   c. Undefined
   d. Undefined

12. _____, or less commonly, denary, usually refers to the base 10 numeral system.
   a. -equivalence
   b. Decimal10
   c. Undefined
   d. Undefined

13. A _____ is a quotient of numbers, like 3⁄4, or more generally, an element of a quotient field.
   a. -equivalence
   b. Fraction10
   c. Undefined
   d. Undefined

14. The word _____ can have three meanings: In _____ theory, a _____ is an abstract object consisting of vertices (or nodes) and edges (or arcs) between pairs of vertices. The _____ of a function f : X ¨ Y is the set of all pairs (x,f(x)) The _____ of a relation, a generalisation of the _____ of a function.
   a. Graph10
   b. -equivalence
   c. Undefined
   d. Undefined

15. A _____ is a multiplicative factor of a certain object such as a variable (for example, the coefficients of a polynomial), a basis vector, a basis function and so on. Usually, the objects and the coefficients are indexed in the same way, leading to expressions such asa1x1 + a2x2 + a3x3 + ... where an is the _____ of the variable xn for each n = 1, 2, 3, ...
   a. Coefficient10
   b. -equivalence
   c. Undefined
   d. Undefined

16. The outcome of a trial is called the _____.
   a. ADE classification
   b. Event10
   c. Undefined
   d. Undefined

17. A _____ is the result of multiplying, or an expression that identifies factors to be multiplied
   a. -equivalence
   b. Product10
   c. Undefined
   d. Undefined

18. A _____ is a well-defined collection of objects considered as a whole.
   a. Set10
   b. -equivalence
   c. Undefined
   d. Undefined

19. _____ is a branch of mathematics which studies structure and quantity. It may be roughly characterized as a generalization and abstraction of arithmetic, in which operations are performed on symbols rather than numbers. It includes elementary _____, taught to high school students, as well as abstract _____ which covers such structures as groups, rings and fields. Along with geometry and analysis, it is one of the three principal branches of mathematics.
   a. ADE classification
   b. Algebra10
   c. Undefined
   d. Undefined

20. _____ (from the Greek words Geo = earth and metro = measure) is the branch of mathematics first popularized in ancient Greek culture by Thales (circa 624-547 BC) dealing with spatial relationships. The earliest beginnings of _____ may be traced to Ancient Egypt
   a. Geometry10
   b. -equivalence
   c. Undefined
   d. Undefined

Chapter 1

1. a	2. a	3. a	4. b	5. b	6. a	7. a	8. a	9. b	10. b
11. b	12. a	13. b	14. a	15. a	16. a	17. b	18. a	19. b	20. b
21. a	22. b	23. a	24. a	25. a	26. a	27. a	28. b	29. b	30. b
31. a	32. b	33. a	34. b	35. b	36. b	37. a	38. a	39. a	40. b
41. a	42. a	43. a	44. a	45. b	46. b	47. b	48. b	49. b	50. b
51. a	52. b	53. b	54. a	55. a	56. a	57. a	58. a	59. a	60. b
61. a	62. a	63. a	64. b	65. a	66. a	67. a	68. b	69. a	70. b
71. b	72. b	73. b	74. b	75. b	76. b	77. a	78. a	79. b	80. b
81. b	82. a	83. a	84. b	85. b	86. a	87. a	88. a	89. b	90. b
91. a	92. b	93. b	94. a	95. a	96. b	97. a	98. a	99. b	100. b
101. b	102. b	103. a	104. b	105. b	106. b	107. a	108. b	109. a	110. b
111. a	112. a	113. b	114. a	115. b	116. a	117. b	118. a	119. a	120. a
121. b	122. a	123. b	124. b	125. a	126. b	127. b	128. a	129. a	130. b
131. b	132. a	133. a	134. b	135. a	136. a	137. a	138. b	139. a	140. a
141. b	142. a	143. a	144. b	145. b	146. b	147. a	148. a	149. b	150. b
151. b	152. b	153. a	154. a						

Chapter 2

1. a	2. a	3. a	4. a	5. b	6. a	7. b	8. a	9. a	10. a
11. a	12. a	13. b	14. a	15. b	16. b	17. b	18. b	19. a	20. b
21. b	22. a	23. a	24. a	25. a	26. b	27. b	28. b	29. b	30. a
31. a	32. b	33. b	34. b	35. a	36. a	37. a	38. a	39. a	40. b
41. b	42. b	43. a	44. b	45. a	46. b	47. b	48. b	49. b	50. a
51. a	52. a	53. b	54. b	55. b	56. a	57. a	58. b	59. b	60. a
61. a	62. a	63. a	64. a	65. a	66. a	67. a	68. b	69. a	70. a
71. a	72. b	73. b	74. b						

Chapter 3

1. a	2. a	3. a	4. b	5. b	6. b	7. a	8. a	9. a	10. b
11. a	12. b	13. a	14. b	15. b	16. a	17. b	18. a	19. b	20. b
21. a	22. b	23. b	24. a	25. b	26. a	27. b	28. a	29. b	30. b
31. b	32. b	33. a	34. a	35. b	36. a	37. b	38. a	39. a	40. b
41. a	42. b	43. b	44. b	45. b	46. a	47. b	48. b	49. a	50. a
51. b	52. a	53. b	54. b	55. a	56. b	57. a	58. a	59. b	60. a
61. a	62. b	63. a	64. b	65. a	66. a	67. a	68. a	69. a	70. a
71. a	72. b	73. b	74. a	75. a	76. a	77. b	78. a	79. b	80. a
81. a	82. b	83. b	84. a	85. a	86. b	87. a	88. b	89. b	90. b
91. a	92. b	93. b	94. b	95. a	96. b	97. b	98. a	99. a	100. a
101. a	102. b	103. b	104. b	105. b	106. a	107. b			

ANSWER KEY

Chapter 4

1. b	2. b	3. b	4. b	5. a	6. b	7. b	8. b	9. b	10. b
11. a	12. a	13. b	14. b	15. b	16. b	17. a	18. b	19. a	20. a
21. a	22. b	23. a	24. b	25. b	26. a	27. b	28. a	29. b	30. a
31. b	32. b	33. b	34. a	35. b	36. a	37. b	38. b	39. a	40. b
41. a	42. a	43. b	44. a	45. b	46. a	47. b	48. a	49. b	50. b
51. b	52. b	53. a	54. a	55. b	56. b	57. b	58. a	59. a	60. b
61. b	62. b	63. b	64. a	65. a	66. b	67. b	68. a	69. b	70. b
71. a	72. a	73. b	74. b	75. b	76. b	77. a	78. b	79. b	80. a
81. a	82. a	83. a	84. a	85. b	86. a	87. b	88. a	89. a	90. a
91. b	92. b	93. b	94. a	95. b	96. a	97. a	98. a	99. b	100. a
101. b	102. b	103. a	104. a	105. a	106. a	107. b	108. a	109. a	110. b
111. b	112. a	113. a	114. a	115. a	116. a	117. b	118. a	119. a	120. b

Chapter 5

1. b	2. a	3. b	4. b	5. b	6. a	7. b	8. a	9. a	10. a
11. a	12. a	13. a	14. a	15. a	16. a	17. b	18. b	19. b	20. b
21. a	22. b	23. b	24. a	25. a	26. b	27. b	28. a	29. a	30. a
31. a	32. b	33. a	34. b	35. a	36. b	37. a	38. b	39. b	40. a
41. b	42. a	43. a	44. b	45. a	46. a	47. b	48. b	49. b	50. a
51. b	52. b	53. a	54. b	55. b	56. b	57. a	58. a	59. a	60. b
61. a	62. a	63. b	64. b	65. b	66. a	67. a	68. a	69. b	70. b
71. b	72. b	73. a	74. a	75. b	76. b	77. a	78. a	79. b	80. a
81. a	82. b	83. b	84. a	85. a	86. a	87. b	88. a	89. b	90. b
91. a	92. b	93. a	94. a	95. a	96. a	97. a	98. a	99. a	100. a
101. b	102. a	103. b	104. b	105. a	106. a	107. a	108. b	109. a	110. a

Chapter 6

1. b	2. a	3. a	4. b	5. b	6. a	7. b	8. b	9. b	10. b
11. b	12. b	13. b	14. a	15. b	16. a	17. b	18. b	19. b	20. b
21. a	22. b	23. b	24. a	25. b	26. b	27. a	28. b	29. a	30. b
31. b	32. b	33. a	34. a	35. a	36. a	37. b	38. a	39. a	40. b
41. a	42. a	43. a	44. a	45. a	46. a	47. a	48. b	49. a	50. a
51. b	52. a	53. b	54. a	55. a	56. b	57. b	58. a	59. b	60. b
61. b	62. a	63. a	64. a	65. b	66. a	67. a	68. b	69. a	70. a
71. b	72. b	73. a	74. a	75. b	76. b	77. b	78. a	79. b	80. a
81. a	82. b	83. a	84. b	85. a	86. b	87. b	88. a	89. a	90. a
91. a	92. b	93. a	94. a	95. b	96. b	97. a	98. b	99. a	100. a
101. b									

Chapter 7

1. b	2. b	3. b	4. a	5. b	6. a	7. b	8. a	9. a	10. b
11. a	12. b	13. b	14. a	15. b	16. b	17. a	18. b	19. b	20. a
21. a	22. b	23. a	24. b	25. a	26. b	27. b	28. a	29. b	30. a
31. b	32. b	33. b	34. a	35. a	36. a	37. a	38. a	39. a	40. a
41. b	42. a	43. a	44. b	45. b	46. b	47. b	48. b	49. b	50. a
51. a	52. a	53. a	54. b	55. b	56. b	57. a	58. a	59. b	60. a
61. a	62. b	63. a	64. a	65. b	66. b	67. b	68. a	69. a	70. b
71. a	72. a	73. b	74. b	75. b	76. b	77. b	78. b	79. b	80. a
81. b	82. b	83. a	84. a	85. b	86. b	87. b	88. a	89. a	90. b
91. b	92. a	93. a	94. b	95. b	96. a	97. b	98. a	99. a	100. a
101. a	102. b	103. a	104. b	105. a	106. b	107. b	108. a	109. a	110. a
111. b	112. b	113. b							

Chapter 8

1. b	2. b	3. b	4. a	5. a	6. a	7. b	8. a	9. b	10. b
11. b	12. b	13. b	14. b	15. a	16. b	17. a	18. a	19. b	20. a
21. a	22. b	23. a	24. a	25. b	26. b	27. b	28. b	29. a	30. b
31. b	32. a	33. b	34. a	35. a	36. b	37. b	38. a	39. b	40. b
41. a	42. a	43. b	44. a	45. a	46. b	47. b	48. b	49. a	50. b
51. b	52. b	53. a	54. b	55. b	56. b	57. b	58. a	59. b	60. b
61. b	62. a	63. a	64. b	65. b	66. b	67. b	68. b	69. b	70. b
71. a	72. b	73. b	74. a	75. b	76. b	77. a	78. b	79. b	80. b
81. a	82. b	83. a	84. a	85. a	86. a	87. b	88. b	89. b	90. a
91. a	92. b	93. b	94. b	95. b	96. a	97. b	98. a	99. b	100. a
101. a	102. b	103. a	104. a	105. b	106. b	107. b	108. a	109. b	110. b
111. a	112. b								

Chapter 9

1. b	2. b	3. a	4. a	5. a	6. a	7. a	8. b	9. a	10. b
11. a	12. b	13. a	14. b	15. a	16. a	17. a	18. a	19. a	20. a
21. a	22. b	23. a	24. a	25. b	26. a	27. a	28. a	29. a	30. b
31. a	32. b	33. a	34. a	35. b	36. a	37. b	38. a	39. a	40. b
41. b	42. a	43. a	44. a	45. b	46. a	47. b	48. a	49. b	50. a
51. a	52. b	53. b	54. b	55. a	56. b	57. a	58. b	59. a	60. b
61. b	62. a	63. a	64. a	65. b	66. a	67. b	68. a	69. b	70. b
71. a	72. b	73. a	74. b	75. a	76. a	77. a	78. b	79. b	80. a
81. a	82. a	83. a	84. a	85. b	86. a	87. a	88. b	89. b	90. a
91. a	92. b	93. a	94. b	95. b	96. a	97. a	98. a	99. b	100. a
101. b	102. a	103. b	104. b	105. a	106. a	107. a	108. b	109. a	110. a
111. b	112. a	113. b	114. a	115. b	116. a	117. b	118. a	119. b	

ANSWER KEY

Chapter 10

| 1. a | 2. b | 3. a | 4. a | 5. b | 6. b | 7. a | 8. a | 9. a | 10. a |
| 11. a | 12. b | 13. b | 14. a | 15. a | 16. b | 17. b | 18. a | 19. b | 20. a |